The
all^ New
Jewish
Quiz
Book

The *all*^ New Jewish Quiz Book

Barbara Spector

The Jewish Publication Society

Philadelphia • Jerusalem
1998

Printed in Canada

Library of Congress Cataloging in Publication Data
Spector, Barbara.
    The all new Jewish quiz book / Barbara Spector.
        p   cm.
    Includes bibliographical references.
    Summary: Miscellaneous information about Jews and Judaism
presented in question and answer format.
    ISBN 0-8276-0594-3
    1. Jews—History—Examinations, questions, etc.—Juvenile
literature. 2. Judaism—Examinations, questions, etc.—Juvenile
literature. [1. Jews—History. 2. Judaism. 3. Questions and
answers.] I. Title.
DS118.5.S64   1997
909'.04924'0076—dc21   96-52516

Typeset by   0198
Book Design Studio II   97 98 99 00 10 9 8 7 6 5 4 3 2 1

For my mother,
SHIRLEY SPECTOR

Acknowledgments

This book came about through the inspiration of two special people: my original editor at the Jewish Publication Society, David A. Adler, who in 1985 had the initial vision for *The Great Jewish Quiz Book* and asked me to write it; and Bruce Black, who as JPS children's book editor in 1994 envisioned a sequel. The society, under the management of Ellen Frankel as editor-in-chief, enabled me to work to make this project a reality. Christine Sweeney handled the editorial project management with care. Rabbi Israel Stein checked my facts and provided helpful suggestions. Special thanks are due to my friends and former colleagues Delores Kaplan and Dolores Verbit for their unwavering enthusiasm and encouragement.

I learned a tremendous amount about the world Jewish community and about journalism and writing in general from my former coworkers at the *Jewish Exponent* in Philadelphia. The work of some of them is referenced as source material for this volume. I also wish to acknowledge my past and present colleagues at *The Scientist* as a source of professional inspiration.

In the course of my research I asked many Jewish organizations to send me photographs and information. Most were more than happy to comply, sending me what I requested and then some. These organizations are listed in the references at the back of this book. I thank them for their generosity.

A great deal of research for this book was conducted at public, university, and synagogue libraries. Particularly helpful to me were the Tuttleman Library at Gratz College in Melrose Park, Pa., and the Clarence L. and Estelle S. Meyers Library of Reform Congregation Keneseth Israel in Elkins Park, Pa. I urge readers to support their local Jewish and public libraries so that future generations of researchers may turn to them to learn major and minor facts about Judaism and other subjects.

With what some would call my characteristic *chutzpah,* I asked friends to take photos to appear in this book. Some of these pictures made it into the finished product; others unfortunately had to end up on the cutting-room floor. Kudos to Ira Band, Judi Goldblatt, Elizabeth Okin Ninyo and Jak Yasar Ninyo, and Edward Silverman for letting me take advantage of them in this way.

Other friends helped by giving or lending me reference materials, providing transportation, and offering quiet, peaceful places to stay while I did my research. For this and more, I say a big thank you to Tim Baradet, Dr. Abraham Fremer, Megan and Steve Golden, Katie Loeb, Ted Micka, Rennie and Krishna Narine, Julie Osler, Jack Prucella, and Seymour Silverberg. This is by no means an exhaustive list; virtually all of my friends and colleagues who knew I was writing this book made some kind of contribution, directly or indirectly. I owe a huge debt of gratitude to everyone who provided moral support, advice, and food while I was immersed in this project, which coincided with a tumultuous time in my personal life.

Most of all, I'd like to thank my mother, Shirley Spector, and my brother, Ken Spector, whose love continues to sustain me from venture to venture.

Barbara Spector

Contents

1. Where in the late Middle Ages would one be likely to encounter a *letz*, a *marshallik*, and a *badḥan*?

(a) at a Jewish wedding; (b) at a Jewish funeral; (c) in a Jewish kitchen; (d) in a ḥeder, or religious school.

2. Who were the *Anusim?*

3. What's a *shulklapper?*

4. What are known to Yemenite Jews as *simonim?*

(a) *tzitzit;* (b) tefillin; (c) *pa'ot;* (d) *dreidels.*

5. What was the *pileum cornutum?*

6. A *shivviti* plaque in a Jewish home is a decorative way of reminding the people who live there to _____.

(a) face east when praying; (b) separate milk from meat; (c) give money to charity; (d) think of God at all times.

7. What's an *almemar?*

(a) an Israeli olive tree; (b) a Yom Kippur prayer; (c) a reader's desk in a synagogue; (d) an almond pastry eaten on Shavuot.

Answers on page 13

8. What is "mitzvah *gelt*"?

9. *Matkot* is a Hebrew name for _____.
(a) the custom of beating willow branches on the seventh day of Sukkot;
(b) the cloth bag used to hold tefillin; (c) a skin treatment using mud from
the Dead Sea; (d) an Israeli beach game in which a rubber ball is hit with
wooden paddles.

10. What's a *nevelah?*

11. What is Habima?
(a) an international organization of pulpit rabbis; (b) a Zionist youth group;
(c) an Israeli political party; (d) Israel's national theater.

12. During an *essen tag,* in a custom from the times of the great yeshivot in Europe,
yeshivah students were welcome to come to a townsperson's home to _____.
(a) eat a meal; (b) study a page of Talmud; (c) choose a marriage partner;
(d) get a haircut.

13. What are *ta'ame neginah?*
(a) matzah crackers made by Manischewitz; (b) hasidic melodies; (c) Torah
trop, or cantillation notes; (d) Purim parties.

14. What's a *hilula?*

(a) the *yahrzeit* of an especially saintly rabbi; (b) a collection of prayers said on festivals and new moon days; (c) an organization of Jewish college students; (d) a punishment to be brought upon the wicked when the Messiah comes.

15. What's a *seudah mafseket?*

(a) another word for the Passover seder; (b) the last meal before a fast; (c) a special meal eaten on Shabbat; (d) the feast of the leviathan that, according to tradition, will be eaten by the righteous when the Messiah comes.

16. What are *taggin?*

(a) a Yiddish name for day-school students; (b) the Hebrew word for bases in the game of baseball; (c) little "crowns" decorating some of the letters in a Torah scroll; (d) the authors of the *Targum,* an Aramaic translation of the Bible.

17. What are *kvitlech?*

(a) matzah balls; (b) people who *kvetch,* or complain, a lot; (c) a food eaten by Iranian Jews on Purim; (d) petitions to God written on little notes and put between the stones of the Western Wall.

18. What is *ḥolov Yisroel?*

19. What's a *shtibl?*
    (a) a small hasidic synagogue; **(b)** a 19th-century Eastern European village;
    (c) a hat worn by hasidic men; **(d)** a wig worn by Orthodox women.

20. What is blessed during *Kiddush Levanah?*
    (a) a shroud; **(b)** the moon; **(c)** yogurt; **(d)** white wine.

**Learning
the Lingo**

12

Learning the Lingo Answers

1. **(a)** at a Jewish wedding. (A *letz* was a jester, a *marshallik* was a master of ceremonies, and a *badḥan* was a buffoon.) 2. Jews throughout history who were forced to convert but who secretly continued to observe at least some Jewish commandments and customs. (The term "Marranos," or, less pejoratively, "conversos," generally refers to Jews who were forcibly converted during the Spanish Inquisition.) 3. A mallet used by the *shammash*, or sexton, in Eastern Europe to knock on house shutters to awaken people for morning prayers. 4. **(c)** *pa'ot* (long, curled sidelocks). 5. A "Jewish hat"—a special horned headdress that Jews were required to wear, by order of the Council of Vienna in 1267, so that they could be recognized from a distance. 6. **(d)** think of God at all times. (A *shivviti* plaque is a wall decoration with the words "I have set *[shivviti]* the Lord before me always" [Ps. 16:8].) 7. **(c)** a reader's desk in a synagogue. (It comes from the Arabic *alminbar*, meaning "platform" or "pulpit.") 8. Money given to someone who is going on a journey to donate to charity upon arrival. (The custom comes from a passage in the aggadic portion of the Talmud that no harm will come to a person involved in doing a mitzvah.) 9. **(d)** an Israeli beach game in which a rubber ball is hit with wooden paddles. 10. A *nevelah*, or "carcass," is an animal that, following an inspection, is found to have not been slaughtered according to the precise ritual, and is therefore forbidden as food. 11. **(d)** Israel's national theater. 12. **(a)** eat a meal. (*Essen tag* means "eating day.") 13. **(c)** Torah trop, or cantillation notes (the musical notes used in the chanting of Torah readings). 14. **(a)** the *yahrzeit* of an especially saintly rabbi. (The term is Aramaic.) 15. **(b)** the last meal before a fast. 16. **(c)** little "crowns" decorating some of the letters in a Torah scroll. 17. **(d)** petitions to God written on little notes and put between the stones of the Western Wall. 18. Milk whose processing has been watched by a Jew to ensure that it has not been mixed with nonkosher fatty substances. 19. **(a)** a small hasidic synagogue. 20. **(b)** the moon. (*Kiddush Levanah*, or the sanctification of the moon, takes place in the first half of the month, after the birth of the new moon, on a night when the moon is visible.)

1. What is the only major Jewish holiday that starts on the first day of the month?

2. According to the Talmud, which holiday is the only one that will still be celebrated after the Messiah comes?
   (a) Yom Kippur; (b) Sukkot; (c) Simḥat Torah; (d) Purim.

3. Why is no blessing for the new moon recited in the month of Tishrei?

4. What are the six holidays mentioned in the Torah (other than Shabbat)?

5. Which Jewish holiday occurs in the first month of the Hebrew calendar?

6. In Temple times, which Hebrew month marked the beginning of the year for the tithing of animals?
   (a) Nisan; (b) Elul; (c) Tishrei; (d) Shevat.

7. The Warsaw Ghetto uprising took place in 1943 on the eve of which holiday?
   (a) Yom Kippur; (b) Simḥat Torah; (c) Pesaḥ; (d) Shavuot.

8. According to tradition, on which night of the week are demons the most powerful?
   (a) Sunday; (b) Tuesday; (c) Thursday; (d) Saturday.

Answers on page 21

9. In the days of the Temple, what was the only festival on which every family (as opposed to the priests) brought a sacrifice?

(a) Rosh Hashanah; (b) Yom Kippur; (c) Pesaḥ; (d) Shavuot.

10. According to the Talmud, on which holiday did Abraham and Sarah conceive Isaac?

(a) Rosh Hashanah; (b) Sukkot; (c) Lag B'Omer; (d) Purim.

11. During which Hebrew month is it customary in some communities to blow the shofar every day?

12. According to the Talmud, the prophet Elijah will not appear to herald the arrival of the Messiah on a Friday. Why not?

13. On which holiday did Jews in the former Soviet Union hold massive demonstrations to protest restrictions on their ability to emigrate?

(a) Rosh Hashanah; (b) Yom Kippur; (c) Simḥat Torah; (d) Purim.

14. The Torah directs that the *omer* be counted at the beginning of the harvest of what type of grain?

(a) wheat; (b) barley; (c) oats; (d) rice.

15. The prayer for dew is introduced in the service on the first day of which holiday?

(a) Rosh Hashanah; (b) Sukkot; (c) Pesaḥ; (d) Shavuot.

16. According to the Talmud, young, marriageable women in ancient Jerusalem held public dances at the conclusion of which holiday?

(a) Pesaḥ; (b) Hanukkah; (c) Yom Kippur; (d) Hoshanah Rabbah.

17. On what holiday is the Scroll of Ecclesiastes read?

(a) Sukkot; (b) Pesaḥ; (c) Shavuot; (d) Tisha B'Av.

18. What is the only holiday (other than Shabbat) on which work related to food preparation and the use of fire is prohibited?

19. What holiday coincides with the start of the rainy season in Israel?

(a) Rosh Hashanah; (b) Sukkot; (c) Tu B'Shevat; (d) Shavuot.

20. In which Hebrew month, according to tradition, will Elijah, and then the Messiah, arrive?

(a) Nisan; (b) Elul; (c) Tishrei; (d) Av.

1. A Jew, Lucius Littauer, will go down in history as the first _____.
   (a) Nobel Prize winner; (b) designated hitter; (c) governor of Kansas;
   (d) college football coach.

2. Who was the first Jew to be named to the rank of U.S. ambassador?
   (a) Felix Frankfurter; (b) Oscar Straus; (c) Henry Morgenthau, Jr.;
   (d) Louis Brandeis.

3. Who was the first native-born Israeli to be elected president of Israel?
   (a) Zalman Shazar; (b) Ephraim Katzir; (c) Yitzhak Navon; (d) Ezer Weizman.

4. Who was the first woman ever to attend the Jewish Theological Seminary?
   (a) Henrietta Szold; (b) Judith Kaplan Eisenstein; (c) Amy Eilberg;
   (d) Susannah Heschel.

5. Dick Savitt was _____.
   (a) the first Jewish tennis player to win at Wimbledon; (b) the first Jewish
   political writer to have a column in the *Washington Post;* (c) a Jewish actor
   who was the first person to star simultaneously in two top-10 hit TV shows;
   (d) the first Jewish talk-show host.

6. The first Jewish U.S. ambassador to Israel was nominated by which president?
   (a) Harry Truman; (b) Ronald Reagan; (c) George Bush; (d) Bill Clinton.

7. Simon Bamberger was the first Jew to be elected governor of Utah in 1916. All but one of the following statements about him are also true. Which statement is false?
(a) He was the first non-Mormon to be governor of Utah; (b) He was the first Democrat to govern the state; (c) He was one of the founders of Utah's first synagogue; (d) He was a founder of Bamberger's department store.

8. Robert Briscoe was the first Jewish _____.
(a) heavyweight boxing champion; (b) conductor of the Boston Symphony; (c) Lord Mayor of Dublin, Ireland; (d) winner of the New York Marathon.

9. In April 1994, Khaled El-Shami arrived in Israel to become the country's first _____ from Egypt.
(a) rabbi; (b) ambassador; (c) postdoctoral student; (d) soccer player.

10. Who was the first person to sign the Jewish National Fund's "Golden Book," an honorary registry that began when JNF was founded at the fifth Zionist Congress in 1901?
(a) Theodor Herzl; (b) Vladimir Jabotinsky; (c) Zvi Hermann Schapira; (d) Aaron David Gordon.

11. In 1626, Manasseh Ben Israel founded the first Hebrew printing house. In what city was it located?
(a) Venice; (b) Amsterdam; (c) London; (d) Paris.

12. In 1873, Sir Julius Vogel became the first Jewish prime minister of which country?
(a) Canada; (b) New Zealand; (c) Australia; (d) Rhodesia.

13. Who was the first woman rabbi in the United States?

14. Which former president of Israel was the first Israeli to be elected to the U.S. National Academy of Sciences?
(a) Chaim Weizmann; (b) Yitzhak Ben-Zvi; (c) Zalman Shazar;
(d) Ephraim Katzir.

15. Florence Prag Kahn was the first Jewish female _____.
(a) member of Congress; (b) university president; (c) medical school graduate;
(d) member of the U.S. Olympic team.

16. In July 1776, Francis Salvador became the first Jew to die in defense of America. He was a captain in the militia of which state?
(a) South Carolina; (b) Pennsylvania; (c) Delaware; (d) Virginia.

17. In 1927, Charles Levine became the first Jew to _____.
(a) have an audience with the Pope; (b) attend Notre Dame University;
(c) get a job at the Ford Motor Co.; (d) fly across the Atlantic.

18. In April 1994, Howard Nevison of New York's Temple Emanu-El became the first Jewish cantor to sing where?

19. Which U.S. president was the first ever to attend a Jewish High Holy Day service?

  (a) Gerald Ford; **(b)** Jimmy Carter; **(c)** Ronald Reagan; **(d)** Bill Clinton.

20. There are three Jews in the Baseball Hall of Fame. Who was the first Jew elected?

To Everything, a Season Answers

1. Rosh Hashanah. **2. (d)** Purim. **3.** Because the new-moon day is a festival (Rosh Hashanah). **4.** Rosh Hashanah, Yom Kippur, Sukkot, Shemini Atzeret, Pesaḥ, and Shavuot. **5.** Pesaḥ. **6. (b)** Elul. **7. (c)** Pesaḥ. **8. (d)** Saturday (after Shabbat has ended). **9. (c)** Pesaḥ. **10. (a)** Rosh Hashanah. **11.** Elul (the last month before the beginning of the new year). **12.** Because the Jews will be preoccupied with preparations for Shabbat. **13. (c)** Simḥat Torah. **14. (b)** barley. **15. (c)** Pesaḥ. **16. (c)** Yom Kippur. **17. (a)** Sukkot. **18.** Yom Kippur. **19. (b)** Sukkot. (The prayer for rain is started on the eighth day of Sukkot and is continued until the first day of Pesaḥ.) **20. (a)** Nisan.

Answers

Trailblazers Answers

1. **(d)** college football coach (Harvard, 1881). **2. (b)** Oscar Straus (named by President William Howard Taft as ambassador to Turkey, after serving two tours there as minister). **3. (c)** Yitzhak Navon (in 1978). **4. (a)** Henrietta Szold. (She was not permitted to graduate as a rabbi.) **5. (a)** the first Jewish tennis player to win at Wimbledon (in 1951). **6. (d)** Bill Clinton (Martin Indyk, confirmed March 3, 1995). **7. (d)** He was a founder of Bamberger's department store. **8. (c)** Lord Mayor of Dublin, Ireland. (He was elected in 1956 and again in 1961.) **9. (c)** postdoctoral student. El-Shami, who had an M.D. from the University of Alexandria, came to the Weizmann Institute of Science in Rehovot to study the use of genetic engineering in cancer therapy. **10. (c)** Zvi Hermann Schapira. Herzl, who had wanted to be first, yielded the honor to Schapira, who conceived the idea to create JNF. **11. (b)** Amsterdam. **12. (b)** New Zealand. **13.** Sally Jane Priesand (ordained in 1972). **14. (d)** Ephraim Katzir (a biochemist and biophysicist who was president of Israel from 1973 to 1978. He was elected to the academy in 1966.) **15. (a)** member of Congress. (A California representative, she was elected to her first term in 1924 and served six subsequent terms.) **16. (a)** South Carolina. **17. (d)** fly across the Atlantic. **18.** At the Vatican. He was performing as part of a Holocaust Remembrance Day concert, singing with an Italian Christian choir. The Pope and 150 Holocaust survivors were in attendance. **19. (d)** Bill Clinton. (The president, who in 1994 was vacationing on Martha's Vineyard, attended a Rosh Hashanah service of the Martha's Vineyard Hebrew Center in Edgartown, Mass., at the invitation of Harvard Law School professor Alan Dershowitz, a member of the congregation.) **20.** Hank Greenberg (1956).

1. Why do *Seliḥot* services traditionally start at midnight?

2. How many blasts of the shofar are sounded on Rosh Hashanah in traditional synagogues?
    (a) 3; (b) 30; (c) 60; (d) 100.

3. Why is the *Hallel,* which is said on all other festivals, not said on Rosh Hashanah?

4. Which angel is in charge of prayer and responsible for the effectiveness of the shofar sounds on Rosh Hashanah?
    (a) Gabriel; (b) Michael; (c) Sandalfon; (d) Metatron.

5. According to some authorities, on the morning of Rosh Hashanah one should not greet friends with the traditional New Year's greeting, "May you be inscribed and sealed for a good year." Why not?

6. Which three-paragraph High Holy Days prayer was written by Rabbi Yohanan ben Nuri in the time of the Roman Empire?
    (a) *Uv'khen;* (b) *Al ḥayt;* (c) *Unetaneh Tokef;* (d) *Ashamnu.*

7. How many times is the word "shofar" mentioned in the Bible?
    (a) 1; (b) 3; (c) 47; (d) 69.

Answers on page 26

8. According to tradition, the "Avinu Malkenu" prayer was written by Rabbi Akiba when the people's prayers for _____ were not answered.

(a) forgiveness; (b) rain; (c) good health; (d) peace.

9. What is the name of the shofar sound that consists of three broken notes?

(a) *teru'ah;* (b) *tekiah;* (c) *shevarim;* (d) *shevarim teru'ah.*

10. Some Jews avoid eating nuts on Rosh Hashanah. Why?

11. Why is it customary to eat a fruit for the first time of the season on the second day of Rosh Hashanah?

12. Which of the following foods is *not* customarily eaten on Rosh Hashanah?

(a) apples dipped in honey; (b) a fish head; (c) ḥallah dipped in salt;
(d) a round ḥallah.

13. What should you do if you forget to insert the *ha-melekh* phrases in the *Amidah* prayers during the Days of Awe?

(a) repeat the prayers using the correct words; (b) do not repeat the prayers;
(c) say a special prayer at the end of the *Amidah;* (d) fast for an additional hour on Yom Kippur.

14. How many sins are mentioned in the *Ashamnu?*
  (a) 13; **(b)** 22; **(c)** 24; **(d)** 26.

15. People who are seriously ill are exempt from the commandment to fast on Yom Kippur. In such circumstances, should they say the regular blessings over food and the grace after meals when they eat on that day?

16. True or false: The talmudic rabbis advocated that those who were particularly penitent fast on the day before Yom Kippur as well as on Yom Kippur itself.

17. True or false: The *Kol Nidre* prayer was written during the time of the Spanish Inquisition, when Jews were forced to publicly convert to Christianity but secretly remained Jews.

18. Why did King Solomon waive the observance of Yom Kippur?
  (a) Because the people had been particularly good in the past year and had not committed any sins; **(b)** To enable the people to continue the dedication celebration for the first Temple; **(c)** Because a plague had swept the land of Israel, making it dangerous to fast; **(d)** To demonstrate the power of the king of Israel.

19. The verse "The Lord is God" is repeated seven times at the conclusion of the Yom Kippur *Neilah* service to acknowledge _____.

    (a) Tishri, the seventh month, when Yom Kippur is observed; **(b)** the seven Noahide laws, which all people, Jewish and gentile, must observe; **(c)** the seven days of the week; **(d)** the seven spheres of heaven that praise God.

20. *Yom Kippur Katan* (small Yom Kippur), when people are to assess their spiritual selves and try to change for the better, is observed _____.

    (a) the day after Yom Kippur; **(b)** the day before Pesaḥ; **(c)** the day before the first day of each Hebrew month; **(d)** the day before one's birthday.

Answers
26

Days of Awe Answers

1. Because, according to tradition, the heavens are most receptive to prayer at that time. **2. (d)** 100.
3. Because Rosh Hashanah is the day of judgment, and it would not be appropriate to recite joyous hymns on such a day. **4. (c)** Sandalfon. **5.** Because the Talmud says that righteous people are inscribed for a good year at the very beginning of the new year; thus, using the greeting after the beginning of the holiday would imply that the friend is not among the most righteous. **6. (a)** *Uv'khen.* **7. (d)** 69. **8. (b)** rain. **9. (c)** *shevarim.*
10. Because *egoz*, the Hebrew word for "nut," has the same numerical value (17) as *ḥayt*, the Hebrew word for "sin." (The *aleph* in *egoz* is counted, although the *aleph* in *ḥayt*, which is not pronounced, is not.)
11. Because, since the two days of the holiday are to be viewed as one long day, there is a question of whether it is appropriate to say the *she-he-ḥeyanu* (the blessing for having reached a joyous occasion) on the second day. Eating a new fruit ensures that the blessing is not being said in vain. **12. (c)** ḥallah dipped in salt. (Although ḥallah is customarily dipped in salt on Shabbat, on Rosh Hashanah the ḥallah is dipped in honey, as are apples, to signify a sweet year rather than one starting with a salty taste. A round ḥallah signifies a complete year. The head of the household in some traditions eats a fish head, saying a blessing that "we will become like a head, not a tail.") **13. (a)** repeat the prayers using the correct words (otherwise, the prayer is not considered authentic). **14. (c)** 24. **15.** Yes. (The *yaaleh v'yavo* prayer for Yom Kippur should be inserted in the grace after meals.) **16.** False. They decreed that part of the commandment to fast is to eat a meal before the fast. **17.** False. It was written centuries earlier, although it was particularly relevant then.
18. (b) To enable the people to continue the dedication celebration for the first Temple. **19. (d)** the seven spheres of heaven that praise God. **20. (c)** the day before the first day of each Hebrew month.

1. What was the only war in which Israel was attacked but didn't retaliate?

2. What was the official goal of the Society for Meliorating the Conditions of the Jews, a 19th-century U.S. organization?
    (a) teaching English to Jewish immigrant children; (b) establishing a Jewish state; (c) improving living conditions in poor Jewish immigrant neighborhoods; (d) converting Jews to Christianity.

3. In May 1942, Zionist leaders, including Chaim Weizmann and David Ben-Gurion, adopted a resolution calling for the establishment of a Jewish state in *Eretz Yisra'el* at a conference held in which New York City hotel?
    (a) the Biltmore; (b) the Plaza; (c) the Essex House; (d) the Pierre.

4. True or false: Novelist Emile Zola's *"J'accuse,"* the now-famous open letter to the president of the French republic, was published on the front page of *L'Aurore* during the court-martial of Alfred Dreyfus in 1894.

5. Jews from which country were smuggled to Israel in the 1970s in a program called "Operation Moses"?
    (a) Yemen; (b) the Soviet Union; (c) Iraq; (d) Ethiopia.

6. The Haganah underground defense force Plugot Maḥatz ("shock troops") was more commonly known by its abbreviated name. What was it?

7. What was the name of the king of Denmark who encouraged the rescue of Danish Jews during the Nazi occupation?

8. Eleazar ben Ya'ir led a group of Jews in what renowned episode in history?
(a) the reunification of the Old City with the rest of Jerusalem; (b) the defense of Masada; (c) the Warsaw Ghetto uprising; (d) the battle at Tel Hai.

9. On Oct. 1, 1990, as a result of threats made by Iraqi president Saddam Hussein, Israel began distributing something to its population. What did the government distribute?
(a) gas masks; (b) Uzis; (c) Bibles; (d) MREs ("meals ready to eat," emergency provisions used by the U.S. military).

10. What heroic deed did Miep Gies perform?
(a) She brought Jewish children from Europe to Palestine during the Holocaust; (b) She obtained diplomatic visas for Jews, enabling them to flee European countries during Nazi occupation; (c) She helped hide Anne Frank and her family in Nazi-occupied Holland; (d) She was a spy who helped gather information to help the Allies liberate the concentration camps.

11. What term was used to refer to the Jewish community of Palestine before the establishment of the State of Israel?
(a) *kvutzah;* (b) *ḥaverim;* (c) *yishuv;* (d) *olim.*

12. In the 1920s, attorney Louis Marshall organized a boycott of a large American company to protest the anti-Semitism of its founder. What was the company?

13. Which one of the following Arab countries did not participate in the fighting during the Six-Day War?
(a) Egypt; (b) Lebanon; (c) Jordan; (d) Syria.

14. In 1992, the French government proclaimed the Jour du Vél d'Hiv to commemorate what event in Jewish history?

15. Which future U.S. president issued an order in 1862 expelling Jews from occupied Tennessee?
(a) Andrew Johnson; (b) Ulysses S. Grant; (c) William Howard Taft;
(d) Benjamin Harrison.

16. All but one of the following U.S. states originally prohibited Jews from voting. Which one is the state that offered full equality to Jews from the beginning?
(a) North Carolina; (b) South Carolina; (c) Maryland; (d) New Hampshire.

17. The 10 lost tribes got lost _____.
(a) after the attack by the Amalekites following the Exodus; (b) when Israel was destroyed by the Assyrians in 722 B.C.E.; (c) after the destruction of the first Temple in 586 B.C.E.; (d) after the destruction of the second Temple in 70 C.E.

18. In July 1938, Franklin Roosevelt brought together 32 nations in Evian, France, to discuss Jewish refugees in Central Europe. Only one of these countries pledged to take in 100,000 Jews. Which one?

(a) Australia; (b) Belgium; (c) Norway; (d) the Dominican Republic.

19. In 1888, publisher Ward McAllister refused to list Jews in his famous directory, noting that "our good Jews might wish to put out a little book of their own—called something else, of course." What was the name of McAllister's book?

(a) *The Social Register;* (b) *Who's Who;* (c) the Yellow Pages; (d) *Bartlett's Familiar Quotations.*

20. During the Persian Gulf War in January 1991, 400 students, administrators, and faculty from which university took a two-week trip to Israel to show their solidarity with the Jewish state during wartime?

(a) Brandeis University; (b) the University of Judaism; (c) Yeshiva University; (d) Notre Dame University.

1. Of the 613 commandments in the Torah, how many deal with food and eating habits?

    (a) 13; (b) 27; (c) 50; (d) 104.

2. What was the first nationally distributed U.S. product to display the "Circle U" symbol—signifying kosher certification—on its label?

    (a) Maxwell House Coffee; (b) Heinz Vegetarian Beans; (c) Coca-Cola;
    (d) Philadelphia Cream Cheese.

3. What does the Jerusalem branch of the Burger King restaurant chain call its Whopper sandwich?

    (a) *K'tzitzah G'dolah;* (b) *Ha-melekh;* (c) Whopper; (d) Vopper.

4. According to Jewish folk tradition, finding a double yolk in an egg is a sign of what?

    (a) good luck; (b) bad luck; (c) financial prosperity; (d) a happy marriage.

5. True or false: Any produce grown in Israel is automatically considered kosher.

6. On the day before Yom Kippur, Hoshanah Rabbah, and Purim, it is customary to eat which food?

    (a) matzah balls; (b) apples; (c) honey cake; (d) *kreplach.*

Answers on page 34

7. Would an observant Jew eat at a Moroccan restaurant that had the word *"cacher"* on its sign?

8. Which one of the following cuts of meat could be kosher?
(a) loin; (b) chuck; (c) flank; (d) shank.

9. What food takes its Yiddish name from the German *der Seelachs?*

10. True or false: Mother's milk is dairy.

11. Which one of the following foods found in a modern supermarket's produce aisle is not mentioned in the Bible?
(a) cucumbers; (b) garlic; (c) onions; (d) parsley.

12. What is the only kosher food product that comes from an unkosher creature?

13. You can tell if an egg is from a kosher bird by looking at it. How?

14. Salt is used with bread at meals in a Jewish home as a reminder of _____.
(a) the offering with Temple sacrifices; (b) the Dead Sea; (c) Lot's wife;
(d) the Israelites' years of slavery in Egypt.

15. The first court license revocation against a kosher butcher in the United States occurred in what year?

    (a) 1796; **(b)** 1897; **(c)** 1925; **(d)** 1942.

16. What food is traditionally served as part of the condolence meal?

    (a) black bread; **(b)** eggs; **(c)** *mandelbrot;* **(d)** chicken soup.

17. Is a severely handicapped person who needs to be fed (and, therefore, does not touch the food) obligated to comply with the ritual washing of the hands before a meal?

18. True or false: The K designation on a product label is a copyrighted symbol and thus guarantees that the item is kosher.

19. A company whose food products are under rabbinical supervision must give something to the *mashgiaḥ,* or kosher inspector. What is it?

    (a) a key; **(b)** a knife; **(c)** a copy of its receipts; **(d)** a contribution to his synagogue.

20. According to Jewish tradition, did Adam eat an apple from the Tree of Knowledge?

Times of Struggle, Times of Triumph Answers

1. The Persian Gulf War of 1990–1991. **2. (d)** converting Jews to Christianity. **3. (a)** the Biltmore. **4.** False. *"J'accuse"* didn't appear until 1898, four years after the court-martial of Dreyfus. **5. (d)** Ethiopia. **6.** Palmaḥ. **7.** King Christian X. (Because of the efforts of the Danish government, about 98 percent of Danish Jews were saved.) **8. (b)** the defense of Masada (72 C.E.). **9. (a)** gas masks. **10. (c)** She helped hide Anne Frank and her family in Nazi-occupied Holland. **11. (c)** *yishuv* ("settlement"). **12.** The Ford Motor Co. **13. (b)** Lebanon. **14.** The rounding up and deporting of French and foreign Jews at the Vélodrome d'Hiver on July 16, 1942. **15. (b)** Ulysses S. Grant. **16. (b)** South Carolina. (North Carolina dropped its voting restrictions in 1868, Maryland in 1825, and New Hampshire in 1876.) **17. (b)** when Israel was destroyed by the Assyrians in 722 B.C.E. **18. (d)** the Dominican Republic. (The start of World War II interfered, and only 1,200 Jews arrived.) **19. (c)** *The Social Register.* **20. (c)** Yeshiva University. (The mission was called "Operation Torah Shield.")

Eat and Enjoy Answers

1. (c) 50. **2. (b)** Heinz Vegetarian Beans. (H.J. Heinz and the United Federation of Orthodox Rabbis collaborated on the design of the logo in 1923.) **3. (d)** Vopper. **4. (a)** good luck. (It is also a sign that a barren woman will become fertile.) **5.** False. There are a number of laws in the Torah pertaining to produce grown in Israel, such as required tithes. T'nuva, the Israeli farmers' cooperative, takes out the required tithe in Israel, but not for its export crop. For this reason, among others, rabbis advise congregants to rely only on kashrut certification for Israeli produce. **6. (d)** *kreplach.* **7.** Yes. "*Cacher*" means "kosher." **8. (b)** chuck. **9.** Lox. The German *der Seelachs* is the name for "salmon." **10.** False. Mother's milk is considered *pareve.* **11. (d)** parsley. (The others are mentioned in Num. 11:5.) **12.** Honey (from the bee). It is not considered part of the bee's body. **13.** The eggs of all kosher birds are pointed at one end, whereas the eggs of nonkosher birds are completely round. **14. (a)** the offering with Temple sacrifices. (After the destruction of the Temple, the home became a sanctuary and the table an altar.) **15. (a)** 1796. **16. (b)** eggs. (Their shape is a symbol of nature's recurring cycle.) **17.** Yes, because it is a religious and not a hygienic ritual. **18.** False. The letter K is neither a copyrighted symbol nor certification that a product is kosher. (On the other hand, the various kosher-certifying organizations have registered trademarks, which cannot be put on a label without their authorization.) **19. (a)** a key. (So he can enter the facility at any hour to make sure that no *treif* products are surreptitiously brought in.) **20.** No. Various rabbis have identified the fruit as a fig, a grape, an *etrog,* a nut, and even wheat, but an apple is not one of the possibilities mentioned.

1. The first Hillel unit was founded in 1923 at which university?
   (a) New York University; (b) the University of Pennsylvania;
   (c) the University of Illinois; (d) the University of Southern California.

2. Which Israeli institution of higher learning was originally known as the Daniel Sieff Research Institute?
   (a) Technion; (b) the Weizmann Institute of Science; (c) Tel Aviv University;
   (d) Hebrew University.

3. The first college degree granted to a Jew in America was conferred upon Judah Monis in 1720. Which school gave Monis the degree?

4. The trustees of which Ivy League school voted in 1770 "that the children of JEWS may be admitted into this Institution and entirely enjoy the freedom of their own Religion, without any Constraint or Imposition whatever"?
   (a) Columbia University; (b) Harvard University; (c) Brown University;
   (d) Dartmouth College.

5. Yeshiva University's Stern College for Women was endowed by Max Stern, who arrived in the United States from Germany penniless in 1928 and made a fortune selling what?
   (a) corsets; (b) shoes; (c) horseradish; (d) birdseed.

Answers on page 39

6. In what year was the first professor of Yiddish appointed at an American institution of higher learning?
(a) 1939; (b) 1947; (c) 1968; (d) 1975.

7. For whom is Israel's Bar Ilan University named?

8. The American Jewish Historical Society is headquartered on the campus of which academic institution?
(a) Yeshiva University; (b) Brandeis University; (c) City College of New York;
(d) Hebrew Union College–Jewish Institute of Religion.

9. True or false: Yeshiva University named its medical school after Albert Einstein while Einstein was still alive.

10. What was the name of Ben-Gurion University before it was renamed after David Ben-Gurion following his death in 1973?

11. The University of Judaism in Los Angeles is affiliated with which movement?
(a) Reform; (b) Conservative; (c) Orthodox; (d) Reconstructionist.

12. Sampson Simson in 1800 became the first Jew to graduate from Columbia College. What was unusual about the commencement address he delivered?

(a) He gave the address in Hebrew; (b) He began by saying the *Shema;*
(c) He wore a *tallit* on the podium; (d) He was booed during the speech.

13. Which Israeli university is the only one that requires all undergraduate and graduate students to complete a Judaic studies program in addition to their major?

14. Which U.S. university since 1989 has recruited for its team several basketball players who have played professionally in Israel and has had its men's team's home games broadcast live in Israel?

(a) Brandeis University; (b) Yeshiva University; (c) the University of Miami;
(d) the University of Connecticut.

15. Which university has on its seal the names of two objects decorating the breastplate of the High Priest in Temple times?

(a) Hebrew University; (b) Brandeis University; (c) Yale University;
(d) Hofstra University.

16. Which university is Israel's largest?

(a) Tel Aviv University; (b) Hebrew University; (c) Ben-Gurion University;
(d) Bar Ilan University.

17. Which university's motto is *"Torah u-Madda"*—"Torah and general knowledge"?
(a) Bar Ilan University; (b) Yeshiva University; (c) Brandeis University;
(d) Hebrew University.

18. What is the oldest institution of Jewish higher learning in the United States?
(a) Gratz College; (b) Yeshiva University; (c) Hebrew Union College;
(d) the Jewish Theological Seminary.

19. Which Ivy League university was the first to appoint a professing Jew as its president?
(a) Yale University; (b) Columbia University; (c) Princeton University;
(d) the University of Pennsylvania.

20. Which institution of higher learning contains Israel's only faculty of aerospace engineering?

Higher Learning Answers

1. (c) the University of Illinois. **2. (b)** the Weizmann Institute of Science. **3.** Harvard College granted Monis a Master of Arts degree. His thesis was a Hebrew grammar book, *Dickdook Leshom Gnebreet* [sic], *A Grammar of the Hebrew Tongue*, which in 1735 became the first Hebrew book printed in America. In 1722, Monis converted to Christianity and was appointed an instructor in Hebrew at Harvard College. **4. (c)** Brown University (then known as Rhode Island College). **5. (d)** birdseed. (His pet-food business eventually became Hartz Mountain Industries.) **6. (b)** 1947 (Max Weinreich at City College of New York). **7.** Rabbi Meir Berlin (Bar Ilan), one of the fathers of the Mizraḥi movement. **8. (b)** Brandeis University. **9.** True. Albert Einstein College of Medicine was named for Einstein on his 74th birthday, on March 15, 1953. He died on April 18, 1955. **10.** University of the Negev, a name it had adopted in 1969. (It opened as the Institute for Higher Education in 1965.) **11. (b)** Conservative. **12. (a)** He gave the address in Hebrew. **13.** Bar Ilan University. **14. (d)** the University of Connecticut. **15. (c)** Yale University *(urim* and *tummim)*. **16. (a)** Tel Aviv University. **17. (b)** Yeshiva University. **18. (c)** Hebrew Union College (established in 1875). **19. (d)** the University of Pennsylvania. (It named Martin Meyerson president in 1970. Penn also appointed the first Jewish woman Ivy League president, Judith Rodin, in 1994. John Kemeny, who was appointed Dartmouth College president six months before Meyerson became Penn's president, acknowledged being of Jewish ancestry but didn't describe himself as Jewish.) **20.** Technion.

1. True or false: It is considered exceptionally pious to continue to eat in a *sukkah* in the rain.

2. By which name is the *etrog* known to botanists?
(**a**) *Citrus judeaea;* (**b**) *Citrus succos;* (**c**) *Citrus medica;* (**d**) *Citrus citronea.*

3. True or false: The Talmud specifies a maximum size for a *sukkah.*

4. Which book of the Bible is recited on the eighth day of Sukkot?
(**a**) Ruth; (**b**) the Song of Songs; (**c**) Daniel; (**d**) Ecclesiastes.

5. The prayer for rain is first recited on which day of Sukkot?
(**a**) the first day; (**b**) the second day; (**c**) the first day of *ḥol hamoed;*
(**d**) the last day.

6. On which day of Sukkot is it customary to wear the white, shroud-like *kittel?*
(**a**) the first day; (**b**) the seventh day; (**c**) the eighth day; (**d**) the ninth day.

7. True or false: Jewish marriages traditionally are not performed during *hol hamoed,* the middle days of Sukkot and Pesaḥ.

Answers on page 48

8. All but one of the following statements about *etrogim* are true. Which is the false statement?

(a) They were the first fruit introduced to Europe from the Orient; (b) They are primarily grown in Florida and California; (c) Their peel was used by ancient Jews in a remedy for snakebite; (d) Their pulp has a sour taste.

9. Is it permissible to eat the fruits and vegetables used to decorate one's *sukkah?*

10. What is the proper way to hold the *etrog* when it is shaken together with the *lulav?*

(a) in the left hand, with the *pitom* (tip) pointing up; (b) in the left hand, with the *pitom* pointing down; (c) in the right hand, with the *pitom* pointing up; (d) in the right hand, with the *pitom* pointing down.

11. Which part of the four species of plants that make up the *lulav* set has neither smell nor taste?

(a) the *etrog;* (b) the *lulav* (palm branch); (c) the *hadas* (myrtle); (d) the *aravah* (willow).

12. The *etrog,* believed to have medicinal properties, was thought of as a remedy for all but one of the following conditions. Which one?

(a) bad breath; (b) poisoning; (c) food cravings during pregnancy; (d) diarrhea.

13. If any one of the four species of a *lulav* set is missing, is it permissible to replace just the one item?

14. Which one of the four species was traditionally used to make wreaths for bridegrooms' heads as well as for the spices used in *havdalah?*
    (a) the *etrog;* **(b)** the *lulav* (palm branch); **(c)** the *hadas* (myrtle); **(d)** the *aravah* (willow).

15. What is the name for the prayers recited on Sukkot during the processions around the synagogue?
    (a) *hakafot;* **(b)** *hoshanot;* **(c)** *Hallel;* **(d)** *halleluyot.*

16. On which day of Sukkot is the *aravah,* or the willow part of the *lulav* set, beaten on the ground until all its leaves fall off?
    (a) the second day; **(b)** the fifth day; **(c)** the seventh day; **(d)** the eighth day.

17. According to tradition, on Hoshanah Rabbah, the seventh day of Sukkot, God delivers a final verdict on something. What is it?

18. True or false: Simḥat Torah is mentioned in the Talmud.

19. How many processions with the Torah through the synagogue customarily take place on Simḥat Torah?

    (a) 3; **(b)** 5; **(c)** 7; **(d)** 10.

20. In some congregations, a lighted candle is placed in the ark on Simḥat Torah when all the Torah scrolls are taken out, or candles are put on the poles of the flags waved in the procession around the synagogue. What do the candles symbolize?

    (a) the light of Torah; **(b)** Hanukkah, the next Jewish holiday; **(c)** daylight;
    (d) Shabbat.

1. When the State of Israel was founded in 1948, its Jewish population was about 650,000. What was its approximate Arab population?
   (a) 520,000; (b) 650,000; (c) 870,000; (d) 980,000.

2. How many Arab armies invaded Israel simultaneously in the 1948 War of Independence?
   (a) 2; (b) 4; (c) 6; (d) 8.

3. How long did Israel's War of Independence last?
   (a) about eight months; (b) about a year and a half; (c) about two years;
   (d) about two and a half years.

4. All but one of the following countries voted in favor of partition of Palestine in the United Nations General Assembly in 1947. Which country was not one of the 33 voting for partition?
   (a) Bolivia; (b) Brazil; (c) Colombia; (d) Guatemala.

5. How many invited guests witnessed President Harry Truman's signing of *de jure* U.S. recognition of Israel?
   (a) 3; (b) 25; (c) 160; (d) a crowd estimated at 1,000.

Answers on page 48

6. Who was the first Ashkenazic chief rabbi of modern Palestine, a man widely respected for building consensus with the secular Socialist Zionist pioneers?

(a) Rabbi Shlomo Goren; (b) Rabbi Abraham Isaac Kook; (c) Rabbi Yisrael Lau; (d) Rabbi Eliahu Bakshi-Doron.

7. The Arab village Umm Lebis was acquired by a group of Jerusalem Jews in 1878. When they settled there, what did they rename it?

(a) B'nei Brak; (b) Kiryat Shemoneh; (c) Petaḥ Tikva; (d) Ein Gedi.

8. Until the mid-19th century, the entire Jewish population of Jerusalem lived within the walls of the Old City. What was the first Jewish community built outside the walls?

(a) Rishon Le-Zion; (b) Mea Shearim; (c) Rehavia; (d) Mishkanot Sha'ananim.

9. What Israeli institution was founded in 1909 by 10 young men and two young women at Um Juni by the Sea of Galilee?

10. Which political leader, in a speech before the United Nations General Assembly on May 14, 1947, said, "The fact that no Western European state has been able to ensure the defense of the elementary rights of the Jewish people, and to safeguard it against the violence of the fascist executioners, explains the aspirations of the Jews to establish their own state. It would be unjust not to take this into consideration and to deny the right of the Jewish people to realize their aspiration"?

(a) David Ben-Gurion; (b) Harry Truman; (c) Andrei Gromyko;
(d) Chaim Weizmann.

11. What was the name of the 1882 pamphlet written by Odessa physician Leo Pinsker urging Jews to take control of their own destiny, which motivated many people to become Zionists?

(a) "Auto-Emancipation"; (b) *"J'accuse"*; (c) "The Jewish State";
(d) "Rome and Jerusalem."

12. Who was Israel's first foreign minister?

(a) Golda Meir; (b) Moshe Sharett; (c) Chaim Weizmann; (d) Yitzhak Rabin.

13. In 1967, when Israeli troops captured East Jerusalem and reached the Western Wall, a shofar was blown to mark the joyous occasion. Who blew the shofar?

(a) Moshe Dayan; (b) President Zalman Shazar; (c) Prime Minister Levi Eshkol; (d) Rabbi Shlomo Goren.

14. In what year did Israel become a member of the United Nations?
(a) 1948; (b) 1949; (c) 1957; (d) 1968.

15. What was the first law ever passed by the Knesset?

16. Who was Israel's first ambassador to the Soviet Union?
(a) Golda Meir; (b) Moshe Sharett; (c) Chaim Weizmann; (d) Yitzhak Ben-Zvi.

17. Why are Israel's pre-1967 borders called the "Green Line"?

18. Who was the famous passenger on El Al's first flight in September 1948?
(a) David Ben-Gurion; (b) Moshe Dayan; (c) Harry Truman;
(d) Chaim Weizmann.

19. What was the political party of Golda Meir and Moshe Dayan?
(a) Likud; (b) Labor; (c) National Religious Party; (d) Tsomet.

20. In the late 1930s, the British-appointed Peel Commission investigated the feasibility of _____.
(a) partitioning Palestine into Arab and Jewish states; (b) transporting Jewish children from Nazi-occupied Eastern Europe to Palestine; (c) establishing a Jewish state in Uganda; (d) liberating concentration camps and transporting Jews imprisoned there to Palestine.

Sukkot: The *Lulav*, the *Etrog*, and More Answers

1. False. It is considered taking God's name in vain to recite a blessing for the *sukkah* if it is raining too hard to eat there comfortably. 2. (c) *Citrus medica*. (The fruit was believed to have medicinal powers.) 3. False. (Restaurants and kibbutzim in Israel build *sukkot* that can hold hundreds of people.) 4. (d) Ecclesiastes. 5. (d) the last day (because rain would interfere with the mitzvah of dwelling in the *sukkah).* 6. (b) the seventh day (Hoshanah Rabbah, when, according to tradition, the divine judgment that began on Rosh Hashanah is concluded). 7. True. Marriages are not performed because they would detract from the joy of the holiday. (In Jewish tradition, mixing two joyous occasions is thought to detract from the joy of each.) 8. (b) They are primarily grown in Florida and California. 9. Not until after the holiday. 10. (a) in the left hand, with the *pitom* (tip) pointing up (the way it grows from the tree). 11. (d) the *aravah* (willow). 12. (d) diarrhea. 13. No. The entire set is disqualified. 14. (c) the *hadas* (myrtle). 15. (b) *hoshanot.* 16. (c) the seventh day. (The custom comes from the Temple ritual of beating the willow branches on the altar as a prayer for rain.) 17. Everyone's fate for the new year. 18. False. The Simḥat Torah custom of ending the Torah cycle and beginning it on the same day started in the 14th century. The associated ceremonies were introduced in the 16th century. 19. (c) 7. 20. (a) the light of Torah.

Building a Jewish State Answers

1. (d) 980,000. 2. (c) 6. 3. (b) about a year and a half (from Nov. 29, 1947, when the United Nations' partition decision was adopted, to June 20, 1949, when the Israel-Syria Armistice Agreement, the last of four agreements with Israel's Arab opponents, was signed). 4. (c) Colombia. (It was one of 10 abstentions.) 5. (a) 3 (Maurice Bisgyer, then executive vice president of B'nai B'rith; Frank Goldman, then international president of B'nai B'rith; and Eddie Jacobson, a friend of Truman's who personally appealed for the president to recognize the new country). 6. (b) Rabbi Abraham Isaac Kook. 7. (c) Petaḥ Tikva. 8. (d) Mishkanot Sha'ananim (1860). 9. The kibbutz (Degania). 10. (c) Andrei Gromyko. 11. (a) "Auto-Emancipation." 12. (b) Moshe Sharett. 13. (d) Rabbi Shlomo Goren (a chief rabbi of Israel and chief military chaplain during the 1967 war). 14. (b) 1949. 15. The Law of Return (saying that all Jews have the right to emigrate to Israel and to become citizens immediately). 16. (a) Golda Meir. 17. Because armistice maps produced after the War of Independence had the borders drawn in green. 18. (d) Chaim Weizmann. (The inaugural flight brought the new country's first president home from Geneva.) 19. (b) Labor. 20. (a) partitioning Palestine into Arab and Jewish states.

1. According to a Jewish legend, 40 days before a baby is born, a proclamation is made in heaven. What is proclaimed at this time?

    (a) the name of the baby about to be born; **(b)** the life span of the baby about to be born; **(c)** whether the baby will grow up to be a good or wicked person; **(d)** the name of the person ordained by God to be the baby's future mate.

2. True or false: In Jewish tradition, children are not named for people who are living.

3. It is customary to plant a cedar tree in celebration of the birth of a boy. What kind of tree is planted to celebrate the birth of a girl?

    (a) cedar; **(b)** cypress; **(c)** olive; **(d)** palm.

4. Who are often asked to be the *kvatter* and *kvatterin,* the people who bring the baby into the room and hand him to the *mohel* before a circumcision?

    (a) a childless couple; **(b)** the baby's grandparents; **(c)** two people who do not know each other; **(d)** people with medical or nursing degrees.

5. Why is the *she-he-ḥeyanu* blessing not said at a *brit milah?*

6. How many coins are paid to a *kohen* to "redeem" a firstborn son at a *pidyon ha-ben* ceremony?

    (a) 2; **(b)** 5; **(c)** 10; **(d)** 40.

Celebrations

49

Answers on page 53

7. True or false: It is impossible for there to ever be more than one firstborn son in a family (and, therefore, for family members to observe more than one *pidyon ha-ben* ritual).

8. The earliest a *pidyon ha-ben* ceremony may be held is on the _____day after the birth of the firstborn son.
(a) 3rd; (b) 8th; (c) 31st; (d) 366th.

9. True or false: Traditional Jews attending a Bar Mitzvah never drive to the service.

10. Of the seven Jewish justices who have served on the U.S. Supreme Court, only one did not celebrate a Bar or Bat Mitzvah. Which one?
(a) Ruth Bader Ginsburg; (b) Benjamin Cardozo; (c) Louis D. Brandeis;
(d) Felix Frankfurter.

11. Who had the first Jewish wedding?
(a) Adam and Eve; (b) Abraham and Sarah; (c) Isaac and Rebecca;
(d) Jacob and Leah.

12. True or false: Jewish tradition discourages double weddings.

13. In a traditional premarital ceremony known as *Kabbalat Kinyan,* the groom pulls a handkerchief out of the hand of the officiating rabbi to symbolize what?
  (a) the groom's acceptance of the terms of the *ketubbah;* (b) the sad times that will occur in the marriage; (c) the couple's obligation to raise Jewish children; (d) the purity of the couple's life together.

14. Among European Jews, siblings are supposed to be married in order of their age. If a younger sister gets married first, what does the older one customarily do as a sign of forgiveness?
  (a) remove the bride's veil after the wedding ceremony; (b) eat the head of a fish; (c) dance barefoot at the wedding; (d) get hoisted by the guests on a chair along with the bride and groom.

15. Who arrives at the huppah first, the groom or the bride?

16. Why is the glass that is broken in a Jewish wedding ceremony traditionally wrapped in a napkin?

17. Why are two cups of wine used in a Jewish wedding ceremony?
  (a) so there is one cup for the bride and one for the groom; (b) to symbolize the joining of two families; (c) so there is one cup for the couple and one cup for Elijah; (d) to symbolize betrothal and marriage, which originally were celebrated as two separate ceremonies.

18. It is traditional for newly married Jewish couples to spend the first seven days after their wedding doing what?

19. How long must a divorced Jewish woman wait before remarrying under Jewish law?

(a) 30 days; (b) 60 days; (c) 90 days; (d) one year.

20. In some German Jewish communities, it was customary for a bride and groom, under the huppah, to give each other gifts of which of the following items?

(a) pots for cooking; (b) chickens; (c) the shrouds in which they eventually would be buried; (d) Shabbat candles.

Celebrations Answers

1. **(d)** the name of the person ordained by God to be the baby's future mate. 2. False. Although Ashkenazim customarily name children only after someone who is deceased, Sephardim frequently name their children in honor of someone who is still alive. 3. **(b)** cypress. (According to custom, when a couple marry, wood from each of their trees is used to make the huppah.) 4. **(a)** a childless couple (because, according to folk belief, the task is said to lead to the bearing of a child). 5. Because of the pain involved to the child circumcised. 6. **(b)** 5. (The amount is commanded in the Bible—Num. 18:16.) 7. False. For example, if a man marries, has a son, then divorces and remarries, and if he and the second wife conceive a son that is her firstborn, then that son also must be redeemed. 8. **(c)** 31st. (Thirty days are regarded as a sign of an infant's full viability.) 9. False. If the Bar Mitzvah is held on Shabbat, a traditional Jew is forbidden to drive. But driving is permissible if the Bar Mitzvah is held whenever the Torah is read on a day other than a Shabbat or holy day. 10. **(c)** Louis D. Brandeis. 11. **(c)** Isaac and Rebecca. 12. True (because in Jewish tradition, mixing two joyous occasions is thought to detract from the joy of each). 13. **(a)** the groom's acceptance of the terms of the *ketubbah*. 14. **(c)** dance barefoot at the wedding. 15. The groom (because the huppah symbolizes the home, and Jewish law calls for the bride to be brought to the groom's home). 16. To avoid injury from pieces of broken glass. 17. **(d)** to symbolize betrothal *(erusin)* and marriage *(nisu'in)*, which originally were celebrated in two separate ceremonies. 18. Attending parties in their honor. (The parties are known as *Shevah Berakhot*, because the seven blessings said under the huppah are incorporated into the grace after meals at these celebrations.) 19. **(c)** 90 days (so that there is no question about who is the father of any children she may subsequently have). 20. **(c)** the shrouds in which they eventually would be buried.

1. Who was the first rabbi in the Western Hemisphere?
(a) Gershom Mendes Seixas; (b) Isaac Leeser; (c) Isaac Aboab de Fonseca;
(d) Aaron Lopez.

2. Who was the first rabbi to open a session of the U.S. Congress with a prayer?
(a) Stephen Wise; (b) Isaac Mayer Wise; (c) Morris J. Raphall;
(d) Joseph Krauskopf.

3. True or false: Isaac Mayer Wise and Stephen S. Wise, both pioneers of the
Reform movement, were relatives.

4. Which renowned 20th-century Orthodox rabbi was known as "the Rav"?
(a) Rabbi Menachem Mendel Schneerson; (b) Rabbi Joseph B. Soloveitchik;
(c) Rabbi Shlomo Carlebach; (d) Rabbi Shlomo Goren.

5. Which rabbi is credited with introducing the confirmation ceremony in the
United States?
(a) Isaac Mayer Wise; (b) David Einhorn; (c) Max Lilienthal;
(d) Mordecai Kaplan.

6. For whom is Yeshiva University's Rabbi Isaac Elchanan Theological Seminary
named?

Answers on page 58

7. Which U.S. rabbinical seminary offered Rabbi Abraham Joshua Heschel a position on its faculty before World War II, thus enabling him to escape Nazi Germany?

(a) Hebrew Union College; (b) the Jewish Theological Seminary;
(c) Yeshiva University; (d) Reconstructionist Rabbinical College.

8. Which Israeli chief rabbi, as a seven-year-old child, was imprisoned in the Buchenwald concentration camp?

(a) Shlomo Goren; (b) Eliahu Bakshi-Doron; (c) Avraham Elkana Kahana-Shapiro; (d) Yisrael Lau.

9. The first Jewish sermon to be published in North America was given in 1773 in Newport, R.I., by Rabbi Haim Isaac Carigal of Hebron, who visited America to collect money for the Jewish community in Palestine. The published version was translated into English. In what language did the rabbi deliver the sermon?

(a) Arabic; (b) Hebrew; (c) Yiddish; (d) Spanish.

10. True or false: The oldest and largest rabbinical seminary in the world is located in America.

11. The only rabbinical seminary in Eastern Europe is located in which city?

(a) Budapest; (b) Moscow; (c) St. Petersburg; (d) Prague.

12. True or false: There are certain mitzvot that can be performed only by rabbis.

13. *New York Times* publisher Adolph S. Ochs was the son-in-law of a noted American rabbi. Which one?
(a) Mordecai Kaplan; (b) Isaac Mayer Wise; (c) David Einhorn; (d) Stephen Wise.

14. What was Rabbi Judah Loew ben Bezalel's famous creation?
(a) the knitted kippah; (b) the cherry hamantasch; (c) the Golem of Prague; (d) the song "Oseh Shalom."

15. Hebrew Union College–Jewish Institute of Religion, a Reform rabbinical seminary, has campuses in four cities: New York, Los Angeles, Jerusalem, and _____.
(a) Philadelphia; (b) Miami; (c) Chicago; (d) Cincinnati.

16. Rabbi Baruch Korff was referred to as "my rabbi" by which U.S. president?
(a) Harry Truman; (b) Richard Nixon; (c) Jimmy Carter; (d) George Bush.

17. Which rabbi and talmudic scholar is pictured on a $1.00 U.S. postage stamp?
(a) Abraham Joshua Heschel; (b) Joseph B. Soloveitchik; (c) Bernard Revel; (d) Isaac Mayer Wise.

The Rabbis' Quiz

56

18. What was the name of the protagonist of Harry Kemelman's mystery *Friday, the Rabbi Slept Late* and its sequels?

(a) Rabbi David Schwartz; (b) Rabbi David Small; (c) Rabbi David Solomon; (d) Rabbi David Steinberg.

19. Orthodox rabbi and scholar Joseph B. Soloveitchik taught at a school located in which of the following cities?

(a) Cleveland, Ohio; (b) Brookline, Mass.; (c) Livingston, N.J.; (d) Monticello, N.Y.

20. Rabbi David Einhorn settled in Baltimore in 1855, but was forced to leave in 1861 because of angry mob protests. What did he do that made people so angry?

The Rabbis' Quiz Answers

1. (c) Isaac Aboab de Fonseca. (He was born a Marrano in Portugal and moved with his family to Amsterdam when he was a child. In 1624 he came to Recife, Brazil, a Dutch colony, to be rabbi of the Jewish community. He returned to Amsterdam in 1654 when the Portuguese recaptured Recife.) **2. (c)** Morris J. Raphall. (He was rabbi of New York's Congregation B'nai Jeshurun. The invocation was given in 1860.) **3.** False. **4. (b)** Rabbi Joseph B. Soloveitchik. **5. (c)** Max Lilienthal (rabbi of the Reform Bene Israel congregation of Cincinnati from 1855 to 1882). **6.** Rabbi Isaac Elchanan Spektor (1817–1896) of Kovno, Lithuania, a leading 19th-century rabbinical scholar. **7. (a)** Hebrew Union College, a Reform seminary. (He moved to the Jewish Theological Seminary, a Conservative institution, in 1945.) **8. (d)** Yisrael Lau. **9. (d)** Spanish. **10.** True (Hebrew Union College–Jewish Institute of Religion). **11. (a)** Budapest. **12.** False. (While in Catholicism, for example, there are certain rituals that can be performed only by priests, there are no Jewish laws that are applicable only to rabbis.) **13. (b)** Isaac Mayer Wise. **14. (c)** the Golem of Prague, which, according to a 16th-century legend, was created to expose a blood-libel plot against the Jews. **15. (d)** Cincinnati (the main campus). **16. (b)** Richard Nixon. (Korff was a staunch defender of Nixon during the Watergate crisis.) **17. (c)** Bernard Revel. (He was the founding president of Yeshiva College. The stamp was issued on Sept. 23, 1986, as part of the "Great American" series.) **18. (b)** Rabbi David Small. **19. (b)** Brookline, Mass. (at the Maimonides School. He also taught at Yeshiva University in New York City.) **20.** He gave sermons advocating the abolition of slavery.

1. True or false: The name "Hanukkah" is mentioned in the Books of Maccabees.

2. According to the interpreters of the Mishnah known as *Amoraim,* what kind of oil was in the flask discovered by the Hasmoneans?
    (a) olive oil; (b) canola oil; (c) vegetable oil; (d) corn oil.

3. True or false: When Judah Maccabee rededicated the Temple, he decreed that the Hanukkah festival be celebrated by the kindling of lights.

4. Which of the following is another name for Hanukkah?
    (a) *Ḥag ha-Asif;* (b) *Ḥag ha-Urim;* (c) *Ḥag ha-Katzir;* (d) *Ḥag ha-Aviv.*

5. Who was the last surviving Maccabee brother?
    (a) Judah; (b) Eliezer; (c) Simon; (d) Jonathan.

6. What was the name of the traitorous High Priest who helped Antiochus find ways to undermine Jewish observance before the Hasmonean revolt?
    (a) Yohanan; (b) Holofernes; (c) Menelaus; (d) Mattathais.

7. The fifth stanza of which Hanukkah hymn gives the entire story of the Maccabean battle and the miracle of the oil in just 24 words?

8. In what year was the first torch lit at Modi'in, birthplace of Judah Maccabee, in a Hanukkah celebration?

    (a) 170 B.C.E.; **(b)** 75 C.E.; **(c)** 1944; **(d)** 1975.

9. True or false: On Hanukkah, Jews are obligated to light one candle on the first night, two on the second, and so on.

10. Is it permissible for a family to light more than one Hanukkah menorah?

11. How do you fulfill the Hanukkah mitzvah of *pirsum ha-nes?*

    (a) by giving gifts to the poor; **(b)** by eating latkes; **(c)** by playing the *dreidel;*
    (d) by putting your Hanukkah menorah by your window or doorway.

12. According to the talmudic rabbis, are women obligated to light Hanukkah lights?

13. True or false: According to Jewish law, it is permissible to read by the light of Hanukkah candles.

14. When is *Zot Hanukkah,* a day considered in some communities to have special significance?

    (a) the first day of Hanukkah; **(b)** the last day of Hanukkah; **(c)** one month before the start of Hanukkah; **(d)** one month after the end of Hanukkah.

15. What do the four letters on the *dreidel* stand for in Yiddish?

16. If a poor person has to make a choice between buying Hanukkah candles or buying Shabbat candles, which type has priority?

17. What food is traditionally eaten at Hanukkah in honor of Judith, who contributed to the Hasmonean victory by killing General Holofernes?
  (a) nuts; (b) dates; (c) coin-shaped chocolates wrapped in gold foil;
  (d) cheese.

18. Which classical composer was undergoing financial difficulties until he saved his career in 1746 by writing an oratorio about a Hanukkah hero?
  (a) Georg Friedrich Handel; (b) Johann Sebastian Bach; (c) Joseph Haydn;
  (d) Wolfgang Amadeus Mozart.

19. The prayer *Al Ha-Nissim* ("we thank You for the miracles") is inserted in the *Amidah* and *birkat hamazon* on Hanukkah and what other holiday?
  (a) Shavuot; (b) Yom ha-Azma'ut; (c) Pesaḥ; (d) Purim.

20. What does a *dreidel* player do when the letter *shin* is showing on the *dreidel?*
  (a) nothing; (b) he or she takes the whole "pot"; (c) he or she takes half the
  "pot"; (d) he or she puts one object into the "pot."

Hanukkah: A Great Miracle Happened There Answers

1. False. **2. (a)** olive oil. **3.** False. His official proclamation was for the event to be marked "with mirth and gladness" (I Macc. 4), but he did not specify any rituals. The candlelighting ritual is rabbinically ordained. **4. (b)** *Ḥag ha-Urim* (the holiday of lights). **5. (c)** Simon. (He was elected ruler and High Priest by the people.) **6. (c)** Menelaus. **7.** "Maoz Tzur." **8. (c)** 1944. **9.** False. The actual religious obligation is only to light one candle per night. (The Talmud says that those who want to beautify the commandment should add an extra candle for each day, a practice that has been taken up by Jews all over the world.) **10.** Yes. Many families use one menorah for each member of the household. **11. (d)** by putting your Hanukkah menorah by your window or doorway. (*Pirsum ha-nes* means "publicizing the miracle.") **12.** Yes, because "they too were included in the miracle" (*Shabbat* 23a). **13.** False. The lights are to be used only for ritual illumination and must not be used for any other purpose, such as reading. **14. (b)** the last day of Hanukkah. (It is considered significant because it is the culmination of the holiday. The name comes from the first words of the Torah reading.) **15.** *Nits* (nothing), *ganz* (everything), *halb* (half), and *shtell-arein* (put some in). **16.** Shabbat candles. According to the fourth-century scholar Rava, they take priority because they are essential for domestic peace. (He said, however, that Hanukkah candles have priority over wine for *kiddush.*) **17. (d)** cheese. (Judith lulled Holofernes to sleep by feeding him a dairy dish.) **18. (a)** Georg Friedrich Handel. (He wrote *Judas Maccabaeus.*) **19. (d)** Purim. **20. (d)** he or she puts one object (usually a coin or a nut) into the "pot."

Answers

62

1. Which one of the Ten Commandments did the rabbis say was the most important?
(a) the first; (b) the fourth; (c) the fifth; (d) the sixth.

2. The origin of the prayer for the government recited on Shabbat morning after the Torah reading can be traced to _____.
(a) the joy over the establishment of the State of Israel; (b) the fear raised by the rise of Nazism; (c) the establishment of the first Jewish congregation in America; (d) a verse in the Book of Jeremiah.

3. How many services each year conclude with the phrase "Next year in Jerusalem"?
(a) one; (b) two; (c) three; (d) six.

4. According to the Talmud, is it a mitzvah to recite a benediction when one is not required?

5. Who are the seven relatives for whom one is obligated to sit *shivah*?

6. True or false: The Torah commands Jewish men to cover their heads.

Answers on page 66

7. What is done to the fringes of a *tallit* when it is buried along with a deceased person?
  (a) nothing—they are left intact; **(b)** they are cut on one corner;
  (c) they are tied in a knot; **(d)** they are dyed blue.

8. True or false: The *tallit* is never worn for evening services.

9. On what occasion is it customary to say, "Now I have a *Kaddish*"?
  (a) upon the death of a close relative; **(b)** upon turning 13 years old;
  (c) upon the birth of one's son; **(d)** on one's deathbed.

10. Why are *mezuzzot* positioned diagonally on a doorpost?
  (a) so people can touch them regardless of how tall they are; **(b)** because the Torah commands that they be positioned diagonally; **(c)** because the slanted position is believed to ward off the evil eye; **(d)** to accommodate the opinions of two dissenting talmudic commentators.

11. What religious practice is known to Sephardim as *annos?*

12. True or false: Some Jews change their tefillin during a prayer service.

13. True or false: The traditional mourning period for a parent is longer than that for a spouse.

14. Should a sanctuary have a *mezuzzah* on its doorpost?

15. True or false: The same kind of parchment should be used for tefillin as is used for a Torah scroll and for a *mezuzzah.*

16. The first record of a minyan is found in _____.
   (a) the Torah; (b) the Prophets; (c) the Talmud; (d) the Dead Sea Scrolls.

17. If you are missing one of the phylacteries of the tefillin set, should you put on just the remaining one?

18. Does traditional Judaism permit the draping of a flag over a casket in honor of the deceased's service to his or her country?

19. It is customary in some communities for mourners, upon their first visit to synagogue following the death, to change their _____.
   (a) seats; (b) yarmulkes; (c) *tallitot;* (d) Hebrew names.

20. After leaving a cemetery, it is customary to _____.
   (a) bow one's head; (b) wash one's hands; (c) remove one's shoes; (d) drink a glass of water.

Laws and Traditions Answers

1. (c) the fifth ("Honor thy mother and thy father." They reasoned that if a child honors his or her parents, the parents will teach him or her all the other commandments.) **2. (d)** a verse in the Book of Jeremiah (29:7: "Seek the welfare of the country where I have sent you into exile; pray to the Lord for it, for your welfare depends on its welfare.") **3. (b)** two (the Pesaḥ seder and the Yom Kippur *Neilah* service). **4.** No. The Talmud considers it taking God's name in vain. **5.** Father, mother, sister, brother, son, daughter, spouse. **6.** False. The practice originated in Roman times. **7. (b)** they are cut on one corner (because the mitzvot signified by the fringes are binding only in this world, and burying someone in a kosher *tallit* would be considered as "mocking the dead," who cannot keep the commandment). **8.** False. There is one occasion—*Kol Nidre*— when the *tallit* is worn in the evening. **9. (c)** upon the birth of one's son. (Sons are obligated to say *Kaddish* for their parents. Although most daughters take this duty upon themselves as well, women are not obligated to do so under traditional Jewish law.) **10. (d)** to accommodate the opinions of two dissenting talmudic commentators (Rashi, who said they should be positioned vertically, and his grandson Rabbenu Tam, who said they should be positioned horizontally). **11.** The observance of *yahrzeit*, or the anniversary of the day of death. **12.** True. (They do it because Rashi and his grandson Rabbenu Tam differed about the sequence of the verses as they appear in the boxes of the tefillin. Some observant Jews, unsure about whose opinion should be followed, compromise by following both opinions.) **13.** True. For a parent, the mourning period is 11 months; for a spouse, sibling, or child, it is 30 days. **14.** A place that is used for prayer is not a dwelling place (it is forbidden to eat there) and therefore is not required to have a *mezuzzah*. However, other rooms in a synagogue that are used for eating and meeting need a *mezuzzah*. **15.** False. According to Maimonides, a Torah scroll should be written on whole parchment, on the side next to the hair of the original hide; tefillin should be written on the exterior part of a split hide, on the side that was next to the animal's flesh; and the *mezuzzah* should be written on the inner part of the split hide, on the side nearer the hair. **16. (a)** the Torah. (In Num. 14:27, the 10 spies—not counting Joshua and Caleb—are referred to as an *edah*, or "congregation.") **17.** Yes. (While one should make every effort to have a complete set, it is preferable to use a partial set rather than none at all.) **18.** Yes. **19. (a)** seats. (It is believed that the custom arose either as a way of pointing out mourners to the congregation, or out of superstition that the Angel of Death might be lurking over their seats.) **20. (b)** wash one's hands (because everyone who enters a cemetery becomes ritually unclean and must undergo ritual purification).

1. Who said, "Your Majesty, the entire State of Israel is shaking your hand," and on what occasion did he say it?

2. What did Solomon Schechter once describe as "a work too varied, too disconnected, and too divergent in its elements, to be concisely defined at all, or to be even approximately described within the limits of an English sentence"?
   (a) the Bible; (b) the Talmud; (c) the *siddur;* (d) the Shulḥan Arukh.

3. Who wrote in her autobiography: "It wasn't just that I decided to go to Palestine. I was so enthusiastic that I influenced a number of other children, some of whom were younger and looked up to me, to go as well"?
   (a) Golda Meir; (b) Hannah Senesh; (c) Henrietta Szold;
   (d) Dr. Ruth Westheimer.

4. Who greeted his wife with the words, "Sorry I'm a little late" when they were reunited after a separation of 12 years (nine of which he had spent in prison)?
   (a) former Soviet Jewish refusnik and activist Natan Sharansky; (b) author and Holocaust survivor Elie Wiesel; (c) Jewish gangster Bugsy Siegel;
   (d) militant Zionist and former Israeli Prime Minister Menachem Begin.

Answers on page 75

5. Who wrote: "American Jews need more chutzpah. Notwithstanding the stereotype, we are not pushy or assertive enough for our own good and for the good of our more vulnerable brothers and sisters in other parts of the world"?

(a) comedian Jackie Mason; (b) comedian and film director Woody Allen; (c) Harvard Law School professor Alan Dershowitz; (d) *New York Times* columnist and former Nixon speechwriter William Safire.

6. Whose last words were "It is good to die for our country"?

(a) Yitzhak Rabin; (b) Joseph Trumpeldor; (c) Yonatan Netanyahu; (d) Hannah Senesh.

7. Who said, "I came to feel that if I, as a Jew, hit a home run, I was hitting one against Hitler"?

8. What Israeli landmark did 20th-century rabbi and philosopher Abraham Joshua Heschel describe as possessing "No comeliness to be acclaimed, no beauty to be relished. But a heart and an ear"?

(a) the Western Wall; (b) Dizengoff Square; (c) Yad Vashem; (d) the menorah outside the Knesset building.

9. In 1492, when the Jews were expelled from Spain, the ruler of which country gave an order to the governors of his provinces "not to refuse the Jews entry nor cause them difficulties, but to receive them cordially"?

(a) England; (b) Italy; (c) Morocco; (d) the Ottoman Empire (Turkey).

10. What famous text begins with these words: "The Land of Israel was the birthplace of the Jewish people. Here their spiritual, religious and national identity was formed"?

(a) the Camp David peace accords; (b) the Balfour Declaration; (c) Israel's Declaration of Independence; (d) Theodor Herzl's *The Jewish State.*

11. The great rabbi and scholar Judah ha-Nasi (135–222 C.E.) said: "I learned much from my teachers, much more from my comrades, and most of all from _____."

(a) "my students"; (b) "my parents"; (c) "myself"; (d) "books."

12. Who wrote in her diary: "I feel that I have a mission. I don't know what my mission is, but I know that I have a responsibility to others"?

(a) Anne Frank; (b) Hannah Senesh; (c) Henrietta Szold; (d) Golda Meir.

13. Which famous Jew told his B'nai B'rith lodge: "Because I was a Jew, I found myself free from many prejudices which restricted others in the use of their intellect; and as a Jew I was prepared to join the opposition and to do without agreement with the 'compact majority'"?

    (a) Albert Einstein; **(b)** Louis Brandeis; **(c)** Sigmund Freud; **(d)** Woody Allen.

14. The leader of which European country, in acknowledging his nation's responsibility for deporting thousands of Jews to Nazi death camps during German occupation, said, "These dark hours forever sully our history and are an insult to our past and our traditions"?

    (a) Austria; **(b)** Luxembourg; **(c)** Poland; **(d)** France.

15. Who wrote a letter requesting that Jewish settlers be required "in a friendly way to depart; praying also most seriously . . . that the deceitful race . . . be not allowed to further infect and trouble this new colony"?

    (a) Peter Stuyvesant; **(b)** William Penn; **(c)** Roger Williams;

    (d) Lord De La Warr.

16. Which Jewish hero's motto was, "If you will it, it is not a dream"?

    (a) Yitzhak Rabin; **(b)** Theodor Herzl; **(c)** Natan Sharansky;

    (d) Judah Maccabee.

17. Who wrote in a letter to a friend: "The main thing is that the dream of my life has come true. I have had the fortune to set my eyes upon Jewish defense in the ghetto in all its greatness"?

18. Which U.S. politician, in a book he authored, wrote that "the Jewish National Fund's tree planting movement continues to serve as a model for what could be accomplished all over the world both in degraded areas of the underdeveloped world and in industrial societies"?
(a) Arlen Specter; (b) Edward Koch; (c) Al Gore; (d) Jimmy Carter.

19. Who wrote: "If a Jew is murdered for no other reason except that he is a Jew, and, had he not been a Jew, he would have remained alive, then it may truly be said that he sacrificed his life *al kiddush ha-Shem,* for the holiness of God"?
(a) Elie Wiesel; (b) Natan Sharansky; (c) Theodor Herzl; (d) Maimonides.

20. Who wrote in his autobiography: "More than ever I saw the affinity between the Jew and the Negro. The Jews had been oppressed for three thousand years instead of three hundred like us, but the rest was very much the same . . ."?
(a) Martin Luther King, Jr.; (b) Sidney Poitier; (c) Sammy Davis, Jr.;
(d) George Washington Carver.

1. Who was the first person in the Bible to thank the Lord?
  (a) Eve; **(b)** Sarah; **(c)** Leah; **(d)** Rachel.

2. Was Moses a *kohen?*

3. According to the Bible, all the known peoples of the world are descended from the three sons of whom?
  (a) Adam; **(b)** Noah; **(c)** Abraham; **(d)** Jacob.

4. Which biblical woman came from the Valley of Sorek?
  (a) Sarah; **(b)** Rebecca; **(c)** Bathsheba; **(d)** Delilah.

5. How long did King David live?
  (a) 40 years; **(b)** 70 years; **(c)** 120 years; **(d)** 900 years.

6. Who blessed Israel with the expression, "How goodly are your tents, O Jacob" (*Mah tovu ohalekha Yaakov*)?
  (a) Balaam; **(b)** Saul; **(c)** Moses; **(d)** Solomon.

7. Which biblical woman's silent prayer, which was heard by God, was said by the rabbis to be an example of how to pray, and thus is the basis for having the silent *Amidah* at the center of the liturgy?
  (a) Rachel; **(b)** Sarah; **(c)** Hannah; **(d)** Ruth.

Answers on page 75

8. According to Rashi, how long did it take Noah to build the ark?
(a) 1 year; (b) 13 years; (c) 70 years; (d) 120 years.

9. Who was the first child to be Jewish from birth?

10. Who was the mother of Jacob's sons Dan and Naphtali?
(a) Jacob's wife Leah; (b) Jacob's wife Rachel; (c) Jacob's concubine Bilhah;
(d) Jacob's concubine Zilpah.

11. How old was Noah when the flood came?
(a) 70 years; (b) 150 years; (c) 600 years; (d) 900 years.

12. Shortly after Cain killed Abel, Eve had another son. Who was he?
(a) Seth; (b) Ham; (c) Enoch; (d) Methuselah.

13. Which priest and scribe led the return of the exiles from Babylonia to rebuild the Temple?

14. When the Israelites finally made it to the Promised Land, 40 years after the Exodus from Egypt, how many members of the generation that left Egypt were still alive?
(a) 40; (b) 12; (c) 10; (d) 2.

15. The Edomites, an enemy of Israel, were the descendants of which person in the Bible?

(a) Amalek; (b) Esau; (c) Moab; (d) Ishmael.

16. Which archangel, who specializes in healing and whose name means "God is healing," visited Abraham to heal him after his circumcision?

17. Who was the father of Nadav and Avihu?

(a) Solomon; (b) Moses; (c) Aaron; (d) Joshua.

18. Amram and Jochebed were the parents of _____.

(a) Zipporah; (b) Rebecca; (c) Naomi; (d) Moses.

19. Who was Solomon's mother?

(a) Merab; (b) Michal; (c) Abigail; (d) Bathsheba.

20. Which male biblical hero, according to Rashi, was very particular about his hairstyle and even used eye makeup?

(a) David; (b) Jacob; (c) Joseph; (d) Samson.

So Tell Me Answers

1. Israeli Prime Minister Yitzhak Rabin said it to King Hussein of Jordan after the two countries signed a peace declaration in October 1994. **2. (b)** the Talmud. **3. (d)** Dr. Ruth Westheimer. **4. (a)** former Soviet Jewish refusnik and activist Natan Sharansky. **5. (c)** Harvard Law School professor Alan Dershowitz. **6. (b)** Joseph Trumpeldor. (He was killed while defending the settlement of Tel Hai.) **7.** Detroit Tigers star Hank Greenberg. **8. (a)** the Western Wall. **9. (d)** the Ottoman Empire (Turkey). **10. (c)** Israel's Declaration of Independence. **11. (a)** "my students." **12. (b)** Hannah Senesh. **13. (c)** Sigmund Freud. **14. (d)** France. (President Jacques Chirac made the statement on July 16, 1995, in ceremonies commemorating the 53rd anniversary of the first mass arrests of 13,000 Jews in Paris on July 16, 1942. When he made the statement, Chirac had been in office for only about two months.) **15. (a)** Peter Stuyvesant (the administrator of New Netherland [New York]. He wrote it in a letter to the Dutch West India Company in 1654). **16. (b)** Theodor Herzl (referring to the building of a Jewish state). **17.** Mordecai Anielewicz, hero of the Warsaw Ghetto uprising. **18. (c)** Al Gore *(Earth in the Balance)*. **19. (d)** Maimonides. **20. (c)** Sammy Davis, Jr.

They're All in the Bible Answers

1. (c) Leah. (She thanked God for the birth of her son Judah in Gen. 29:35.) **2.** No. He was a Levite. **3. (b)** Noah. **4. (d)** Delilah. **5. (b)** 70 years. **6. (a)** Balaam (Num. 24:5). **7. (c)** Hannah. (She prayed for a son and became the mother of Samuel.) **8. (d)** 120 years. **9.** Isaac. **10. (c)** Jacob's concubine Bilhah. **11. (c)** 600 years. **12. (a)** Seth. **13.** Ezra. **14. (d)** 2 (Joshua the son of Nun and Caleb the son of Jephunneh). **15. (b)** Esau. **16.** Rafael. **17. (c)** Aaron. **18. (d)** Moses. **19. (d)** Bathsheba. **20. (c)** Joseph.

1. True or false: All Jews celebrate Purim on the same day.

2. In what chapter of the megillah is Haman's name first mentioned (and, therefore, the *gragers* first sounded)?
  (a) the first; **(b)** the second; **(c)** the third; **(d)** the fourth.

3. True or false: Purim takes place on the anniversary of the Jews' military victory.

4. Why do some people write Haman's name on the soles of their shoes before the megillah reading?

5. King Ahasuerus' minister Memucan advised him to get rid of _____.
  (a) Queen Vashti; **(b)** Haman; **(c)** Queen Esther; **(d)** the wine in the palace.

6. True or false: Esther fasted on the day before Purim.

7. What did Esther do on the night after her fast?

8. Haman was a descendant of which biblical villain?
  (a) Pharaoh; **(b)** King Agag; **(c)** Balak; **(d)** Chedorlaomer, King of Elam.

Answers on page 79

9. According to tradition, what happened to Haman's grandchildren after he and his 10 sons were hanged?
(a) they were hanged as well; (b) they fled from Shushan; (c) they went blind;
(d) they converted to Judaism.

10. True or false: As it is read, the megillah is customarily rolled up, like a Torah scroll.

11. The talmudic tractate that is devoted to Purim is called _____.
(a) *Megillah;* (b) *Grager;* (c) *Hamantasch;* (d) *Adloyada.*

12. What is *Purim torah?*
(a) the Bible reading for the holiday; (b) the custom of making fun of Jewish tradition on Purim; (c) a pastry eaten on Purim; (d) the name of the carnival held in Israel on Purim.

13. On Purim, to fulfill the mitzvah of *matanot le-evyonim,* each Jewish household is obligated to send aid to at least how many poor people?
(a) 1; (b) 2; (c) 5; (d) 10.

14. True or false: The Hebrew phrases *barukh Mordecai* (blessed be Mordecai) and *arur Haman* (cursed be Haman) add up to the same number in *gematria,* the system of totaling up the numeric equivalent of Hebrew letters.

15. The word "hamantaschen" comes from which language?
(a) Hebrew; (b) Aramaic; (c) Yiddish; (d) Arabic.

16. Because the miracle of Purim occurred outside the land of Israel, the _____ is not chanted on the holiday.
(a) *Hallel;* (b) *Amidah;* (c) *birkat hamazon;* (d) *Shema.*

17. Why is it customary to eat a dish made out of chickpeas on Purim?

18. A poppy-seed mixture is first mentioned as a Purim food in a medieval poem by _____.
(a) Solomon ibn Gabirol; (b) Judah ha-Nasi; (c) Abraham ibn Ezra; (d) Maimonides.

19. How does one fulfill the Purim mitzvah of *mishloah manot?*
(a) by giving *tzedakah;* (b) by eating a big meal; (c) by drinking wine; (d) by sending gifts.

20. According to the Talmud, which rabbi, upon finding himself on Purim in a small town that didn't have a megillah, wrote the whole text from memory?
(a) Rabbi Akiba; (b) Rabbi Hillel; (c) Rabbi Meir; (d) Rabbi Judah ha-Nasi.

Purim: Making Merry Answers

1. False. According to the megillah, while other communities celebrated on the 14th of Adar, the Jews of Shushan were not out of danger until the 14th and could not celebrate until the 15th. Therefore, in Israel all cities that were walled from the time of Joshua celebrate Purim on the 15th of Adar, and the others celebrate it on the 14th. (Tel Aviv's Purim is on the 14th; Jerusalem's is on the 15th.) **2. (c)** the third. **3.** False. Purim takes place on the day after the anniversary of the victory. **4.** So that they can "rub out" Haman's name by rubbing their shoes on the floor during the appropriate points in the megillah reading. **5. (a)** Queen Vashti. (According to a midrash, Memucan is the same as Haman.) **6.** False. Esther fasted for three days, right after she found out about the decree against the Jewish people. According to the Talmud, her fast occurred in the month of Nisan, the last day of which was on Pesaḥ. Jews observe the Fast of Esther on the day of the battle between the Jews and their would-be conquerors. **7.** She had a banquet in honor of King Ahasuerus, to which she also invited Haman. **8. (b)** King Agag (the Amalekite whose life was spared by Saul in I Sam. 15:9. Because of the relationship, the biblical passage exhorting Israel to remember the evil deeds of the Amalekites is read on the Shabbat before Purim). **9. (d)** they converted to Judaism. (Some of the talmudic rabbis were said to be their descendants.) **10.** False. It is customary to fold the megillah like a letter, because of the many proclamations delivered as missives or letters in the Purim story. **11. (a)** *Megillah.* **12. (b)** the custom of making fun of Jewish tradition on Purim. **13. (b)** 2. (The rabbis interpreted the plural form of *matanot le-evyonim* in Es. 9:22 as meaning that aid should be given to at least two people.) **14.** True (502). **15. (c)** Yiddish. (It means "Haman's pockets.") **16. (a)** *Hallel.* **17.** Because, according to tradition, Esther ate only beans and peas while she lived in Ahasuerus' palace so as not to violate the laws of kashrut. **18. (c)** Abraham ibn Ezra. **19. (d)** by sending gifts. **20. (c)** Rabbi Meir (a disciple of Akiba).

1. What is the title of the poem by Jewish-American writer Emma Lazarus whose lines are inscribed on the pedestal of the Statue of Liberty?
(a) *Give Me Your Tired, Your Poor;* (b) *The Huddled Masses;* (c) *The New Colossus;* (d) *The Golden Door.*

2. What, according to the Bible, is the first thing that God said was "not good"?

3. What was the seven-branched menorah in the Temple made of?
(a) silver; (b) gold; (c) bronze; (d) copper.

4. Which of the following is *not* another name for the Ladino language?
(a) Judeo-Spanish; (b) Spaniolish; (c) Castiliano; (d) Sephardish.

5. *Prenumeranten* lists, cited by Jewish genealogists as especially valuable to people tracing their roots, are lists of people who _____.
(a) were born in the local shtetl; (b) were deported by the Nazis; (c) ordered copies of a book before it was published; (d) were enrolled in the local yeshivah.

6. According to the Bible, what was the retirement age for Levites serving in the Temple?
(a) 40; (b) 50; (c) 70; (d) 80.

For Mavens Only

80

Answers on page 87

7. How many countries accept a *get* in lieu of a civil divorce?

8. Chabad, a hasidic sect, gets its name from an acronym for three Hebrew words meaning _____.
    (a) "wisdom, understanding, knowledge"; **(b)** "friendship, covenant, laws";
    (c) "holidays, home, religion"; **(d)** "classroom, blessing, door."

9. True or false: According to the Bible, when, in the first act of creation, God said, "Let there be light," God was speaking of the sun and the moon.

10. *Aviv, Ziv, Etanim,* and *Bul* are biblical names for four _____.
    (a) seasons; **(b)** months; **(c)** birds; **(d)** descendants of Noah.

11. Which noted American Jewish businessman, along with his wife, sank on the *Titanic* in 1912?
    (a) Isidor Straus; **(b)** Adam Gimbel; **(c)** Nathan Straus; **(d)** Levi Strauss.

12. What was the first language that the Hebrew Bible was translated into?
    (a) Aramaic; **(b)** Arabic; **(c)** Greek; **(d)** Latin.

13. True or false: When the Israelites left Egypt, they did not take much material wealth with them.

14. What was the name of the second airlift bringing Ethiopian Jews to Israel in 1991—nearly all of those who were not brought to the Jewish state in the first airlift in 1984?

(a) Operation Moses; (b) Operation Solomon; (c) Operation Exodus; (d) Operation Ezra.

15. What's a *chelmer chochem?*

16. The Holy of Holies in the first Temple housed the two tablets of the Ten Commandments. What did the Holy of Holies in the second Temple contain?

17. In what book of the Tanakh does the word "kosher" first appear?

(a) Exodus; (b) Leviticus; (c) Psalms; (d) Esther.

18. According to Jewish tradition, when the dead are resurrected, what part of the body will be resurrected first?

(a) the head; (b) the heart; (c) a vertebra of the spine; (d) the knees.

19. At the beginning of the 20th century, the garment industry was the biggest employer of Jews in the United States. Which industry was the second largest employer of Jews?

(a) the tobacco industry; (b) the food-service industry;
(c) the banking industry; (d) the railroad industry.

20. Which biblical mountain is also called Mount Horeb, Mount Paran, and the Mountain of God?

    (a) Mount Moriah; **(b)** Mount Sinai; **(c)** Mount Nebo; **(d)** Mount Ararat.

1. Which Israeli city was called the "city of the future" by Theodor Herzl?
    (a) Tel Aviv; (b) Jaffa; (c) Safed; (d) Haifa.

2. What is Israel's tallest mountain?
    (a) Mount Scopus; (b) Mount of Olives; (c) Mount Meron; (d) Mount Hermon.

3. The cornerstone for which Israeli institution was laid on July 24, 1918?
    (a) the first branch of Bank Hapoalim; (b) the Hebrew University; (c) the Shrine of the Book; (d) the Shalom Tower.

4. Ahuzat Bayit was the original name of which Israeli city?
    (a) Tel Aviv; (b) Netanya; (c) Haifa; (d) Eilat.

5. In which Jerusalem neighborhood would one find the Neturei Karta, a group of ultra-religious, anti-Zionist Jews?
    (a) Kiryat Shmuel; (b) Katamon; (c) Mea Shearim; (d) Beit Hakerem.

6. What kind of tree constitutes approximately 80 percent of Israel's planted species?
    (a) the olive tree; (b) the pine tree; (c) the cedar tree; (d) the cypress tree.

Answers on page 87

7. Which Israeli city was founded in the late 19th century by a group of agricultural pioneers, the Ḥovevei Zion, who named it after a quote from the Book of Hosea?

(a) Petaḥ Tikva; (b) B'nei-Brak; (c) Ramat Gan; (d) Kfar Sabba.

8. Which city boasts Israel's only subway?

(a) Tel Aviv; (b) Haifa; (c) Jerusalem; (d) Rehovot.

9. Approximately how high is the Western Wall?

(a) 23 feet; (b) 46 feet; (c) 54 feet; (d) 72 feet.

10. Kiryat Shmoneh—"the City of Eight"—is named in memory of eight pioneers who were killed while defending which Jewish settlement?

(a) Zikron Yaakov; (b) Petaḥ Tikva; (c) Tel Hai; (d) Rishon L'Zion.

11. Which Israeli site is the lowest point on the earth's surface?

12. Which religion has its world center in Haifa?

13. The Temple in Jerusalem was located atop which mountain?

(a) Mount Hermon; (b) Mount Nebo; (c) Mount Moriah; (d) Mount of Olives.

14. Which Israeli town is mentioned in the Book of Joshua, was the residence of Rabbi Akiba, and has a street named after him?

  (a) Beth Shean; **(b)** B'nei-Brak; **(c)** Ashkelon; **(d)** Akko.

15. Which city of ancient Palestine, site of a World War I battle in which British forces defeated the Turks, is believed by Christians to be the location where Armageddon will take place at the "end of days"?

  (a) Akko; **(b)** Nazareth; **(c)** Tiberias; **(d)** Meggido.

16. Which region of Israel encompasses 60 percent of the country's land?

  (a) the Jordan Valley; **(b)** the Negev; **(c)** the Valley of Jezreel; **(d)** the Plain of Sharon.

17. The Kings of Israel Square in downtown Tel Aviv was renamed to honor _____ after his death.

  (a) Yitzhak Rabin; **(b)** Moshe Dayan; **(c)** John F. Kennedy; **(d)** Albert Einstein.

18. Which Israeli city was known in Latin as Aila?

19. True or false: The Western Wall is a remnant of the Temple.

20. What are two other names for the Sea of Galilee?

For Mavens Only Answers

1. (c) *The New Colossus*. 2. The fact that Adam was alone. "It is not good for man to be alone. I will make a helpmate for him" (Gen. 2:18). 3. (b) gold. (It was carved out of one ingot.) 4. (d) Sephardish. 5. (c) ordered copies of a book before it was published. (In return for paying in advance—and to honor their contributions to scholarship—their names were published in the book. *Prenumeranten* is Yiddish for "prior numbers.") 6. (b) 50 (Num. 8:25-26). 7. One—Israel. 8. (a) "wisdom, understanding, knowledge" *(ḥokhmah, binah, da'at)*. 9. False. The sun and the moon were not created until the fourth day. 10. (b) months. 11. (a) Isidor Straus. (Straus, along with his brother Nathan, owned Macy's department store in New York. Isidor Straus's wife, Ida, died along with him in the tragedy.) 12. (c) Greek (the Septuagint, a translation done primarily by the Egyptian community for the benefit of Greek-speaking Jews, completed by the third century B.C.E.). 13. False. According to Exod. 12:36, "they despoiled the Egyptians." The Midrash notes that the Egyptians showered them with gifts because they were glad to be rid of them. 14. (b) Operation Solomon. (The first was called Operation Moses.) 15. A "wise man of Chelm," or a foolish sage. (The town of Chelm in Poland was legendary in Jewish lore for the foolish behavior of its inhabitants.) 16. Nothing (it was an empty room), because the tablets were lost amid the destruction of the first Temple. 17. (d) Esther. (It appears twice more in Ecclesiastes). 18. (c) a vertebra of the spine (one of the lower vertebrae, called the *luz* and said to be indestructible). 19. (a) the tobacco industry. 20. (b) Mount Sinai.

You'll Find It in Israel Answers

1. (d) Haifa. 2. (c) Mount Meron. 3. (b) the Hebrew University (on Mount Scopus). 4. (a) Tel Aviv. 5. (c) Mea Shearim. 6. (b) the pine tree. 7. (a) Petaḥ Tikva (Hos. 2:17). 8. (b) Haifa (the Carmelit). 9. (c) 54 feet. 10. (c) Tel Hai. (The city was established in 1950 on the site of Halsa, a village used by the Arabs as their base for the attack on Tel Hai.) 11. The Dead Sea valley. 12. Baha'i. 13. (c) Mount Moriah. 14. (b) B'nei-Brak (Jos. 19:45). 15. (d) Meggido. 16. (b) the Negev. 17. (a) Yitzhak Rabin. (The square was the site of Rabin's assassination.) 18. Eilat. 19. False. It is actually a remnant of the retaining wall around the Temple. 20. Lake Tiberias and Yam Kinneret.

1. Which one of the following stories does *not* appear in the Book of Genesis?
   (a) Noah's becoming drunk after leaving the ark; **(b)** Abraham's smashing the idols in his father's shop; **(c)** Lot's wife turning into a pillar of salt while look-ing at the destruction of Sodom; **(d)** Esau's selling his birthright to Jacob.

2. True or false: The Torah has always been read in a one-year cycle.

3. *Perek Shirah,* a collection of songs of praise to God, is attributed to _____.
   (a) Moses; **(b)** King Solomon; **(c)** King David; **(d)** insects, birds, and animals.

4. Which book of the Tanakh includes a verse that contains all the letters of the Hebrew alphabet?
   (a) Genesis; **(b)** Habakkuk; **(c)** Psalms; **(d)** Esther.

5. Which book of the Torah contains the greatest number of letters?
   (a) Genesis; **(b)** Exodus; **(c)** Leviticus; **(d)** Numbers.

6. How many times do the Ten Commandments appear in the Torah?

7. True or false: The city of Nazareth is mentioned in the Tanakh.

8. Which book of the Tanakh contains the longest verse?
   (a) Genesis; **(b)** Leviticus; **(c)** Psalms; **(d)** Esther.

Answers on page 91

9. True or false: The Torah contains one passage that, in traditional congregations, is read at night, and is never read on Shabbat.

10. Of the 613 commandments, how many are negative?
   (a) 153; (b) 248; (c) 365; (d) 582.

11. True or false: There is a tractate of the Mishnah that contains no laws.

12. Does one need to have attained Bar or Bat Mitzvah age in order to be called to recite the haftarah?

13. The word *teku* in the Talmud indicates _____.
   (a) the end of the folio; (b) an unresolved dispute; (c) a situation in which capital punishment is called for; (d) a quotation from Rabbi Akiba.

14. Which book of the Tanakh contains the shortest as well as the longest chapter?
   (a) Leviticus; (b) Obadiah; (c) Psalms; (d) Proverbs.

15. Which book of the Hebrew Bible contains the longest word?
   (a) Deuteronomy; (b) Isaiah; (c) Malachi; (d) Esther.

16. In southern Germany in the 13th century, illustrated religious texts depicted people with animals' heads. Why?

17. In which book of the Bible does the word "amen" occur for the first time?
    (a) Genesis; (b) Numbers; (c) I Samuel; (d) Psalms.

18. The Hebrew letter that appears the least frequently in the Torah is _____.
    (a) the final *peh;* (b) the final *kof;* (c) the final *mem;* (d) the final *nun.*

19. What is the only book of the Hebrew Bible in which Satan appears?
    (a) Genesis; (b) Judges; (c) Job; (d) Ecclesiastes.

20. The Zohar—the most famous work of Kabbalah (Jewish mysticism)—is written in which language?
    (a) Hebrew; (b) Arabic; (c) Ladino; (d) Aramaic.

**Sacred
Readings
and Writings**

Sacred Readings and Writings Answers

1. (b) Abraham's smashing the idols in his father's shop. (This is a rabbinical legend.) **2.** False. Until the time of the Gaonim of Babylonia (6th to 11th centuries), it had been read only in a three-year cycle.
3. (d) insects, birds, and animals. (*Perek Shirah* contains six chapters, one of which may be recited on each weekday.) **4. (d)** Esther (3:13). **5. (a)** Genesis (It has 78,084 letters. Exodus has 63,529, Leviticus has 44,790, Numbers has 63,530, and Deuteronomy has 54,892). **6.** Twice (in Exod. 20:2–14 and Deut. 5:6–18). **7.** False. It is mentioned several times in the Christian Bible as the place where Jesus grew up but is not mentioned in the Hebrew Bible or the Talmud. **8. (d)** Esther (8:9—43 Hebrew words). **9.** True (the end of the Torah, read on Simḥat Torah, which deals with the death of Moses). **10. (c)** 365. (There are 248 positive commandments.) **11.** True. (*Pirke Avot,* or *Ethics of the Fathers*). **12.** No. A child as young as seven who can recite the haftarah properly may be called to do so. **13. (b)** an unresolved dispute. (The word, meaning "let it stand," has been interpreted as an abbreviation for "The Tishbite [Elijah] will solve all doubts and perplexities.")
14. (c) Psalms. (The shortest chapter is Ps. 117. The longest chapter is Ps. 119.) **15. (b)** Isaiah. (The word is *Mahershalalḥashbaz* [Is. 8:3], a coined term comprising four words meaning "speedy booty, sudden spoils.")
16. To comply with the biblical injunction against depicting human figures. **17. (b)** Numbers. **18. (a)** the final *peh.* (It appears 834 times in the more than 300,000 letters of the Torah.) **19. (c)** Job. **20. (d)** Aramaic.

1. In what year did Maxwell House Coffee begin distributing haggadot?
    (a) 1934; **(b)** 1948; **(c)** 1955; **(d)** 1962.

2. According to folk tradition, a person who eats one of the items on the seder plate the day after the seder will have his or her wishes fulfilled. What is the lucky food?
    (a) the shank bone; **(b)** the haroset; **(c)** the roasted egg; **(d)** the bitter herb.

3. True or false: All fermented food is prohibited during Pesaḥ.

4. True or false: If there are no children present at a seder, no one has to ask the Four Questions.

5. Which of the following items is *not* included in the category of *kitniyot,* foods that are not eaten by Ashkenazic Jews on Pesaḥ?
    (a) corn; **(b)** peas; **(c)** beans; **(d)** garlic.

6. True or false: It is a violation of Jewish law to feed *ḥametz* to one's pets during Pesaḥ.

7. Which item on the seder plate was introduced first, the roasted egg or the *karpas?*

8. Which one of the following items is not eaten at the seder because it commemorates the paschal lamb, which was forbidden to be eaten outside of Jerusalem?

(a) *karpas;* (b) haroset; (c) *maror;* (d) *zeroah.*

9. A mixture of flour and water that takes more than _____ minutes to bake is assumed to have become leavened and is not kosher for Passover.

(a) 3; (b) 7; (c) 18; (d) 30.

10. What did the ancient Hebrews do with the leftovers of the paschal lamb?

11. When the first seder occurs on a Saturday, when is the search for *hametz* conducted?

(a) Thursday night; (b) Friday afternoon; (c) Saturday evening, just before the seder; (d) Sunday.

12. Why are bread crumbs hidden around the home before the search for *hametz?*

13. Why is a feather used to sweep away the crumbs in the search for *hametz?*

14. According to commentaries on the haggadah, the baby goat in the song "Ḥad Gadya" symbolizes what?

(a) God; (b) the Jewish people; (c) Moses; (d) the firstborn son.

15. True or false: In order for a seder to be valid under Jewish law, the exact wording of the Four Questions as given in the haggadah must be used.

16. The first independent printed haggadah was issued in 1482. In what country was it published?
(a) Italy; (b) Spain; (c) England; (d) Morocco.

17. Which book of the Bible mentions Pharaoh's chariot in its first chapter and is read in the synagogue on Pesaḥ?
(a) Daniel; (b) Job; (c) the Song of Songs; (d) Ecclesiastes.

18. A day on the Jewish calendar known as *Pesaḥ Sheni* (the second Passover) occurs when?
(a) on the second day of Pesaḥ; (b) on the second day of Sukkot; (c) one month after Pesaḥ; (d) on the second day of every month.

19. Which one of the following cannot be *kashered* for Pesaḥ?
(a) china; (b) an oven; (c) silverware; (d) glass.

20. In one ancient custom, to commemorate the way the Hebrews left Egypt, the leader and seder participants passed the *afikoman* around _____.
(a) with their hands behind their backs; (b) from mouth to mouth; (c) under the table; (d) on their shoulders.

Pesaḥ: Enacting the Exodus Answers

1. (a) 1934. **2. (c)** the roasted egg. **3.** False. Only fermented grain products are forbidden. Other fermented consumables (such as wine) are permitted. **4.** False. If the only seder participants are a husband and wife, the wife asks the questions; if all the participants are scholars, they have to ask each other. Even if a person has a seder alone, he or she asks the questions. **5. (d)** garlic. (*Kitniyot,* or legumes, are grains from which bread can be made.) **6.** True. (One is forbidden to derive any benefit from *ḥametz* during the holiday.)
7. *Karpas.* It was introduced in the first century, before the destruction of the Temple. The egg is a commemorative food that was introduced after the destruction of the Temple. **8. (d)** *zeroah* (the roasted shank bone). **9. (c)** 18. **10.** There weren't any. According to tradition, it was forbidden to have leftovers; the entire lamb had to be eaten. (Thus, the people organized themselves into groups to ensure that there were enough people to finish the animal.) **11. (a)** Thursday night. (The search ordinarily occurs on the night before the first seder, but it cannot be conducted on Shabbat.) **12.** To ensure that the blessing said before the search will not be recited in vain. **13.** So that no person is contaminated by touching a crumb of leaven. **14. (b)** the Jewish people. (The animals and objects that attack it signify enemies of the Jews; in the end, God will bring peace.) **15.** False. According to the Talmud, these questions are only a suggestion; it reports several seders in which other questions were asked. **16. (b)** Spain. **17. (c)** the Song of Songs. **18. (c)** one month after Pesaḥ. (According to Num. 9:6–13, any person who, because of ritual impurity, could not offer the Pesaḥ sacrifice on the 14th of Nisan should offer it one month later, on the 14th of Iyyar. Some people commemorate the day by eating matzah.) **19. (a)** china. (It is too porous and absorbent for removal of *ḥametz.*)
20. (d) on their shoulders (to commemorate the Hebrews' exodus from Egypt with "their kneading troughs wrapped in clothes upon their shoulders" [Exod. 12:34]).

Answers

1. This is the emblem of the State of Israel. What type of branch is depicted?
(a) a date-palm branch; (b) an olive branch;
(c) a willow branch; (d) a cypress branch.

2. What event of Jewish interest took place on the site of this building at the corner of Montgomery Street and Columbus Avenue in San Francisco on Sept. 26, 1849?
(a) the first Jewish religious services in the city; (b) the first meeting of B'nai B'rith; (c) the opening of San Francisco's first kosher butcher shop; (d) the opening of the first store owned by Jewish jeans maker Levi Strauss.

Answers on page 102

3. Which company manufactures this plane and all other El Al jets?
  (a) Boeing;
  (b) Lockheed;
  (c) McDonnell-Douglas;
  (d) Airbus.

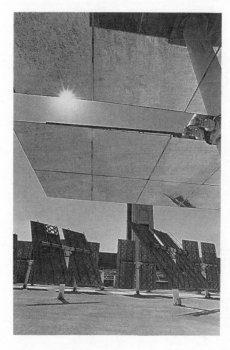

4. Where in Israel can one find this solar tower?
  (a) on the campus of the Hebrew University;
  (b) on the campus of the Technion; **(c)** on the
  campus of the Weizmann Institute of Science;
  (d) on the campus of Bar Ilan University.

5. What is this contemporary ritual object?

6. This is the oldest synagogue building in America. What is its name?
(a) Congregation Shearith Israel in New York City; (b) Congregation Rodeph Shalom in Philadelphia; (c) Congregation Mikveh Israel in Philadelphia; (d) the Touro Synagogue in Newport, R.I.

7. This is a collection of works by which renowned Yiddish author?

(a) Isaac Bashevis Singer;
(b) S. An-Ski;
(c) Sholem Aleichem;
(d) Yehoash.

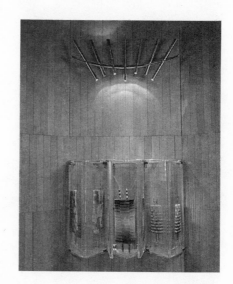

8. This unusual Torah ark and Eternal Light, designed by Israeli artist Yaacov Agam, can be found on a campus of _____.

(a) Yeshiva University;
(b) the Jewish Theological Seminary;
(c) Reconstructionist Rabbinical College;
(d) Hebrew Union College–Jewish Institute of Religion.

9. Is this an Israeli *dreidel?*

**The Great
Photo Quiz**

100

10. What was the inspiration for the design of this synagogue, Beth Sholom Congregation in Elkins Park, Pa., by Frank Lloyd Wright?

    (a) a *Magen David;* **(b)** Mount Sinai;
    (c) the map of the State of Israel; **(d)** the biblical description of the Temple.

11. Shown here is the campus of which university?
  (a) Hebrew University;
  (b) Yeshiva University;
  (c) the University of Judaism;
  (d) Brandeis University.

12. This building on New York City's Fifth Avenue is the former family home of banker and philanthropist Felix M. Warburg and his wife, Frieda Schiff Warburg. What facility of Jewish interest is housed in the building today?
  (a) B'nai B'rith headquarters; **(b)** Congregation Ansche Chesed;
  (c) the Consulate of Israel; **(d)** the Jewish Museum.

The Great Photo Quiz Answers

1. (b) an olive branch. Photo credit: Embassy of Israel **2. (a)** the first Jewish religious services in the city. (Forty Jews gathered for Yom Kippur services in a second-floor room in a store that stood on this location. A plaque on the building commemorates the site.) Photo credit: Judi Goldblatt **3. (a)** Boeing. Photo credit: El Al Israel Airlines Ltd. **4. (c)** on the campus of the Weizmann Institute of Science (in Rehovot). Photo credit: Weizmann Institute of Science **5.** A seder plate (created by Linda Gissen, 1990). Photo credit: National Museum of American Jewish History, Philadelphia **6. (d)** the Touro Synagogue in Newport, R.I. Photo credit: Society of Friends of Touro Synagogue **7. (b)** S. An-Ski (Volume I of *Fun eybigen kval,* or *From the Eternal Spring,* published simultaneously in Vilna, Warsaw, and New York in 1922). Photo credit: YIVO Institute for Jewish Research **8. (d)** Hebrew Union College–Jewish Institute of Religion, at the Minnie Petrie Synagogue, Brookdale Center, New York. (The ark is the gift of Michael and Jeanny Roth. The Eternal Light is the gift of Hannah Hofheimer in memory of her beloved husband, Henry.) Photo credit: Hebrew Union College–Jewish Institute of Religion **9.** No. Israeli *dreidels* say פה or פ, instead of שמ (there) or ש. This is a cast silver reproduction of an 18th-century Eastern European *dreidel.* Photo credit: National Museum of American Jewish History, Philadelphia. **10. (b)** Mount Sinai. Photo credit: Beth Sholom Archives, Elkins Park, Pa. **11. (c)** the University of Judaism (in Los Angeles). Photo credit: University of Judaism **12. (d)** the Jewish Museum. Photo credit: The Jewish Museum, New York, under the auspices of The Jewish Theological Seminary of America

1. Who was the first king of Israel?
   (a) David; (b) Solomon; (c) Saul; (d) Rehoboam.

2. In what year was the first Jewish school in America established?
   (a) 1682; (b) 1731; (c) 1838; (d) 1910.

3. In what year was the first Jewish Lord Mayor of London elected?
   (a) 1855; (b) 1905; (c) 1960; (d) 1975.

4. The *Myrtilla,* a ship owned by early Jewish Philadelphian Nathan Levy, brought which U.S. landmark to Philadelphia from England?

5. The second Jewish settlement in the American colonies was located in what city?
   (a) New York; (b) Philadelphia; (c) Newport, R.I.; (d) Charleston, S.C.

6. Which of the following sects is the ancestor of today's Jews?
   (a) Pharisees; (b) Sadducees; (c) Essenes; (d) Dead Sea sect.

7. The two Roman emperors who destroyed Jerusalem were Titus and _____.
   (a) Julius Caesar; (b) Hadrian; (c) Octavian; (d) Constantine.

Answers on page 107

8. Which ruler established the Pale of Jewish Settlement in Russia?
(a) Czar Nicholas II; (b) Catherine the Great; (c) Czar Alexander II;
(d) Czar Alexander I.

9. The 18th-century opponents of Hasidism were called _____.
(a) *apikoros;* (b) *tzaddikim;* (c) *misnagdim;* (d) *haskalah.*

10. Lionel de Rothschild fought for 11 years—from 1847 to 1858—for the right to do what?
(a) take the oath of office in the British Parliament as a Jew; (b) own a vineyard; (c) inherit his father's money; (d) lend money to Christians.

11. Which Roman emperor promised the Jews that he would restore Jerusalem and the Temple?
(a) Licinius; (b) Theodosius II; (c) Julian; (d) Constantine.

12. Which group of American settlers called themselves the "Christian Israelites" and were referred to by historian James Truslow Adams as "in spirit . . . Jews not Christians"?

13. In the Dutch colony of New Netherland (later New York), Jews were not allowed to work in any trade except one. What was the exception?
(a) tailor; (b) butcher; (c) teacher; (d) baker.

14. The first book printed in what is now the United States was an English translation of one of the books of the Bible, including many Hebrew passages. It was the first use of Hebrew type in the Western Hemisphere. Which book of the Bible was it?

    (a) Genesis; **(b)** Job; **(c)** Psalms; **(d)** Proverbs.

15. How many Jewish congregations were there in New York City in the year 1800?

    (a) 1; **(b)** 5; **(c)** 10; **(d)** 25.

16. In what year was a separate Hebraic section established at the Library of Congress?

    (a) 1800; **(b)** 1870; **(c)** 1914; **(d)** 1945.

17. In what year did the Board of Governors of the Reform movement's Hebrew Union College first vote on the issue of ordaining women as rabbis?

    (a) 1923; **(b)** 1942; **(c)** 1965; **(d)** 1972.

18. Which of the following monarchs issued edicts granting Jews complete freedom of religion and exemption from military service because it would pose conflicts with observance of Shabbat and kashrut?

    (a) Charlemagne; **(b)** Julius Caesar; **(c)** Henry VIII; **(d)** Louis XIV.

19. After the destruction of Jerusalem, in which city was the Sanhedrin (Jewish Supreme Court) located?

    (a) Safed; **(b)** Tiberias; **(c)** Yavneh; **(d)** Cairo.

20. In what year were the Dead Sea Scrolls discovered?

    (a) 1925; **(b)** 1947; **(c)** 1955; **(d)** 1968.

In Olden Days

In Olden Days Answers

1. (c) Saul. **2. (b)** 1731 (the Yeshivah Minchat Areb, an all-day school in New York City). **3. (a)** 1855 (Sir David Salomons). **4.** The Liberty Bell. **5. (c)** Newport, R.I. (Jews arrived there in 1658.) **6. (a)** Pharisees. (The other sects died out after the second Temple was destroyed.) **7. (b)** Hadrian. **8. (b)** Catherine the Great. **9. (c)** *misnagdim* (Hebrew for "opponents.") **10. (a)** take the oath of office in the British Parliament as a Jew (with his head covered and with the Jewish Bible). **11. (c)** Julian. (He was defeated in battle by Persia in 363 C.E., and thus was unable to fulfill his promise.) **12.** The Puritans. (While they probably never met any Jews, they saw England as a modern Egypt, thought of King James I as another Pharaoh, compared their voyage to America to the crossing of the Red Sea, and looked upon New England as the Promised Land.) **13. (b)** butcher. **14. (c)** Psalms (*The Whole Booke of Psalmes Faithfully Translated into English Metre*, known as *The Bay Psalm Book*, 1640). **15. (a)** 1. (Congregation Shearith Israel was the only synagogue in the city from its founding in 1654 until 1825.) **16. (c)** 1914. (The Library, however, was collecting works in Semitic languages from its inception in 1800.) **17. (a)** 1923. (Hebrew Union College student Martha Neumark petitioned the faculty for permission to officiate at High Holy Days services in 1921, prompting the board and the Central Conference of American Rabbis [CCAR] to debate the issue of ordaining women. While CCAR voted in 1922 that women "cannot justly be denied the privilege of ordination," the college's board voted against the change on Feb. 27, 1923. The first Reform woman rabbi was ordained in 1972.) **18. (b)** Julius Caesar. **19. (c)** Yavneh. **20. (b)** 1947.

Answers

107

1. The oldest Jewish house of worship in continuous use under the American flag is located where?
    (a) Newport, R.I.; (b) New York City; (c) St. Thomas, Virgin Islands;
    (d) San Juan, Puerto Rico.

2. Ohel Leah is the name of a synagogue built in 1900 by Sir Jacob Sassoon, scion of a wealthy Sephardic family, in what city?
    (a) London; (b) Istanbul; (c) Hong Kong; (d) Marrakech.

3. What is the better-known name of Congregation Jeshuat Israel in Newport, R.I.?

4. The historic Bevis Marks Synagogue in London is named after _____.
    (a) a wealthy benefactor; (b) the street where it is located; (c) the congregation's first rabbi; (d) a Hebrew phrase.

5. Where is the oldest synagogue in the Western Hemisphere located?
    (a) Newport, R.I.; (b) St. Thomas, Virgin Islands; (c) Recife, Brazil;
    (d) Curaçao.

6. Which of the following is not part of a synagogue?
    (a) Holy ark; (b) Eternal Light; (c) altar; (d) reader's desk.

Answers on page 116

7. The first synagogue to open with official approval in Spain since the expulsion of the Jews in 1492 was dedicated in what year?

(a) 1750; (b) 1823; (c) 1950; (d) 1967; (e) 1978.

8. In the synagogue discovered at Masada, which direction does the ark face?

(a) east; (b) west; (c) north; (d) south.

9. True or false: In the 19th century, many synagogues maintained decorum during services by imposing fines on congregants.

10. At the Mikveh Israel synagogue in Savannah, Ga., in the 1800s, in order to maintain decorum, a rule was passed decreeing that no one could be called to the Torah who was wearing _____.

(a) boots; (b) no necktie; (c) a blue shirt; (d) a yarmulke in a color other than black.

11. Which of the following statements is true?

(a) The synagogue came into existence after the destruction of the second Temple; (b) The synagogue functioned simultaneously with both the first and second Temples; (c) The synagogue functioned simultaneously with the second Temple, but had not yet been established at the time of the first Temple.

12. According to rabbinical authorities, all synagogues must have which one of the following architectural features?

(a) a basement; (b) both a front and a back door; (c) windows; (d) a stone floor.

13. The first Ashkenazic congregation in the Western Hemisphere was established in which city?

(a) Philadelphia; (b) New York; (c) Providence, R.I.; (d) Charleston, S.C.

14. Which historic U.S. synagogue contains a tangible reminder of its early congregants' Marrano past—a secret stairway leading from the *bimah* to the basement?

(a) Congregation Shearith Israel in New York City; (b) the Touro Synagogue in Newport, R.I.; (c) Mikveh Israel Congregation in Philadelphia; (d) Congregation Rodeph Shalom in Philadelphia.

15. New York City's Congregation Shearith Israel has been in existence under the flags of how many nations?

(a) two; (b) three; (c) four; (d) five.

16. How many U.S. synagogues were there at the time of George Washington's presidential inauguration?

(a) one; (b) three; (c) six; (d) ten.

17. Which Italian city boasts a beautiful synagogue, built in 1882 in the Moorish style, that survived near-destruction by the Nazis during World War II as well as a devastating flood in 1966?

    (a) Venice; **(b)** Rome; **(c)** Naples; **(d)** Florence.

18. Reform Temple Beth-el, the oldest congregation to be chartered in the state of Florida, was founded in 1878 in which city?

    (a) Miami; **(b)** Palm Beach; **(c)** Boca Raton; **(d)** Pensacola.

19. The largest synagogue in the world is located in which city?

    (a) Budapest; **(b)** Prague; **(c)** New York; **(d)** Moscow.

20. How many synagogues did architect Frank Lloyd Wright design in his lifetime?

    (a) 1; **(b)** 2; **(c)** 10; **(d)** 27.

1. In what year did *Fiddler on the Roof* open on Broadway?
   (a) 1959; (b) 1964; (c) 1972; (d) 1980.

2. Which character on the Fox television show *The Simpsons* is Jewish?
   (a) Marge Simpson; (b) Otto the school bus driver; (c) Moe the bartender;
   (d) Krusty the clown.

3. Which actress played the lead in the Broadway show *Yentl?*
   (a) Barbra Streisand; (b) Anne Bancroft; (c) Tovah Feldshuh; (d) Carol Kane.

4. Which Jewish actor, an ardent supporter of Israel known for his portrayal of Tevye in *Fiddler on the Roof,* also played a German officer in the movie *The African Queen* and originated the role of Baron Von Trapp in *The Sound of Music?*
   (a) Zero Mostel; (b) Herschel Bernardi; (c) Topol; (d) Theodore Bikel.

5. The character named Oogie on *Reḥov Sum-Sum,* an Israeli version of *Sesame Street,* is the counterpart of which character on the U.S. version of the TV show?
   (a) Cookie Monster; (b) Oscar the Grouch; (c) Ernie; (d) Big Bird.

6. Which actor began his career on the Yiddish stage at age nine and won an Emmy Award for portraying a TV lawyer at age 72?
   (a) Jack Klugman; (b) Ed Asner; (c) Fyvush Finkel; (d) Abe Vigoda.

Answers on page 116

7. Which actress moved to a kibbutz in Israel at age 16 and returned to the United States to make TV commercials before getting her big break by landing a role as Wonder Woman's little sister?

    (a) Debra Winger; **(b)** Carol Kane; **(c)** Jill St. John; **(d)** Fran Drescher.

8. Which Jewish comedian, describing his nose job, said "I cut off my nose to spite my race"?

    (a) Groucho Marx; **(b)** Buddy Hackett; **(c)** Milton Berle; **(d)** Lenny Bruce.

9. Who directed *Shoah,* the 1985 two-part, nine-hour documentary chronicling the memories of people who lived through the Holocaust?

    (a) Louis Malle; **(b)** Ingmar Bergman; **(c)** Claude Lanzmann;
    (d) Milos Forman.

10. Which of the following television series featured a Passover episode?

    (a) *The Simpsons;* **(b)** *Rugrats;* **(c)** *Garfield and Friends;* **(d)** *The Critic.*

11. Which star of *Gone With the Wind* was Jewish?

    (a) Vivien Leigh; **(b)** Clark Gable; **(c)** Olivia de Havilland; **(d)** Leslie Howard.

12. How many Oscars did the Steven Spielberg film *Schindler's List* win?

    (a) four; **(b)** five; **(c)** six; **(d)** seven.

13. In what year did the television mini-series *Holocaust* air?
   (a) 1972; **(b)** 1978; **(c)** 1983; **(d)** 1987.

14. In the opening scene of the animated film *An American Tail,* the family of Fievel Mousekewitz gives him a _____ that had been in the family for three generations as a Hanukkah present.
   (a) book; **(b)** hat; **(c)** coat; **(d)** watch.

15. Two high school classmates from Cleveland, Jerry Siegel and Joe Shuster, created a comic-book character that would later become the hero of a TV show and movie series. Which one?

16. Which Yiddish performer did the vocal gags on Spike Jones's recording "Cocktails for Two" and was the father of an Oscar- and Tony-award-winning actor?
   (a) Mickey Katz; **(b)** Paul Muni; **(c)** Herschel Bernardi; **(d)** Jacob Adler.

17. Who starred in *Crossing Delancey,* a 1988 film about a young New York woman whose Jewish grandmother arranges for her to meet a man through a marriage broker?
   (a) Carol Kane; **(b)** Amy Irving; **(c)** Barbra Streisand; **(d)** Kate Capshaw.

18. Which clarinetist and big-band leader got musical training at the age of 10 at a New York synagogue and the next year joined the boys' club band at Jane Addams's Hull House?

19. Which jazz trumpet player, who was a member of Charlie Parker's band and is portrayed in the Clint Eastwood film *Bird,* got his start as a musician by playing the bugle in a Jewish war veterans' youth band?
   (a) Max Kaminsky; **(b)** Red Rodney; **(c)** Ruby Braff; **(d)** Ziggy Elman.

20. Which jazz saxophonist, from a poor Jewish home in the Bronx, started the bossa-nova craze with his recording of "Desafinado"?
   (a) Stan Getz; **(b)** Lee Konitz; **(c)** Al Cohn; **(d)** Bud Freeman.

A Place to Pray Answers

1. (c) St. Thomas, Virgin Islands (the Hebrew Congregation of St. Thomas, founded in 1796). **2. (c)** Hong Kong. **3.** The Touro Synagogue. **4. (b)** the street where it is located. **5. (d)** Curaçao. (Congregation Mickve Israel marked its 250th anniversary in 1981.) **6. (c)** altar. (Although this term is sometimes incorrectly used, there cannot be an altar in a Jewish place of worship until the Temple is rebuilt and sacrifices are resumed.) **7. (d)** 1967. **8. (b)** west. (Jerusalem is west of Masada.) **9.** True. For example, fines were imposed for inexcusable absences or for leaving before the conclusion of prayers. **10. (a)** boots. **11. (c)** The synagogue functioned simultaneously with the second Temple, but had not yet been established at the time of the first Temple. **12. (c)** windows. (The tradition comes from Dan. 6:11, which describes how Daniel prayed by windows facing Jerusalem. Ber. 34b warns against praying in a room without windows.) **13. (a)** Philadelphia (Congregation Rodeph Shalom, originally known as the Hebrew German Society, Rodeph Shalom, founded in 1795). **14. (b)** the Touro Synagogue in Newport, R.I. **15. (b)** three (Dutch, for a decade after its founding in 1654; British, for a century; and American). **16. (c)** six (in Newport, R.I.; New York; Charleston, S.C.; Philadelphia; Savannah, Ga.; and Richmond, Va.). **17. (d)** Florence. **18. (d)** Pensacola. **19. (c)** New York. (Temple Emanu-El, at Fifth Avenue and 65th Street, completed in September 1929, with a frontage of 150 feet on Fifth Avenue and 253 feet on 65th Street. The sanctuary proper can accommodate 2,500 people. When all its facilities are in use, more than 6,000 people can be accommodated.) **20. (a)** 1 (Beth Sholom Congregation in Elkins Park, Pa.).

Show Biz Answers

1. (b) 1964. **2. (d)** Krusty the clown. **3. (c)** Tovah Feldshuh. (She was nominated for a Tony Award for the role.) **4. (d)** Theodore Bikel. **5. (a)** Cookie Monster. (*Oogiyah* is Hebrew for "cookie.") **6. (c)** Fyvush Finkel. (He won his Emmy for his role as Douglas Wambaugh on *Picket Fences*.) **7. (a)** Debra Winger. **8. (c)** Milton Berle. **9. (c)** Claude Lanzmann. **10. (b)** *Rugrats*. **11. (d)** Leslie Howard (born Leslie Stainer). **12. (d)** seven (including best picture and best director). **13. (b)** 1978. **14. (b)** hat. **15.** Superman. (The pair produced the comic strip for 10 years, but when they signed their first contract in 1938 for $130, they signed away all the rights and thus never profited from Superman merchandise. The "S" on Superman's chest stood for their last names.) **16. (a)** Mickey Katz. (Katz was assistant conductor for Spike Jones and His City Slickers. His son is Joel Grey, star of *Cabaret.)* **17. (b)** Amy Irving. **18.** Benny Goodman. **19. (b)** Red Rodney (Robert Chudnick). **20. (a)** Stan Getz.

1. True or false: According to the Bible, Shavuot commemorates the giving of the Torah at Mount Sinai.

2. If Pesaḥ begins on a Tuesday, what day of the week will the first day of Shavuot be?
(a) Monday; (b) Tuesday; (c) Wednesday; (d) Thursday.

3. Which biblical figure, according to tradition, was born and died on Shavuot?
(a) Moses; (b) Aaron; (c) Jacob; (d) David.

4. Why are the three days before Shavuot called the "Three Days of Limitation" or the "Three Days of Preparation"?

5. On the three days preceding the giving of the Torah, the Israelites were forbidden to approach which holy site closely?
(a) the Temple Mount; (b) Mount Sinai; (c) Rachel's tomb;
(d) the burning bush.

6. In some communities, it is traditional to light 150 candles in the synagogue on Shavuot to symbolize the 150 _____.
(a) chapters in the Book of Psalms; (b) pieces of jewelry used to make the Golden Calf; (c) children of Israel present when Moses came down from Mount Sinai; (d) stars in the sky.

Answers on page 121

7. On Shavuot, it is traditional to visit which mountain?
(a) Mount Zion; (b) Mount Herzl; (c) Mount Meron; (d) Mount Scopus.

8. Which of the following is *not* another name for Shavuot?
(a) the Feast of Weeks; (b) *Ḥag ha-Katzir;* (c) *Yom ha-Bikurim;*
(d) *Z'man Simḥatenu.*

9. True or false: A megillah is read on Shavuot.

10. In many European Jewish towns, Shavuot was the time when young children began to do what?
(a) get their hair cut; (b) study Hebrew; (c) wear *tzitzit;* (d) drink wine.

11. According to a mystical tradition, prayers have an especially good chance of reaching God on Shavuot eve because something happens to the sky. What is said to happen?
(a) lightning strikes; (b) the stars twinkle especially brightly; (c) the heavens open; (d) the sky falls.

12. What was the wave-offering, presented at the Temple altar by the High Priest on behalf of the Israelites?
(a) a willow branch; (b) a fish; (c) a handkerchief; (d) two loaves of bread.

13. The Shavuot service includes the chanting of an 11th-century Aramaic poem about the grandeur of God, the greatness of God's deeds, and the rewards for the righteous in the world to come. What is the name of the poem?

(a) *Addir Hu;* (b) *El Adon;* (c) *Akdamut;* (d) *Yedid Nefesh.*

14. The custom of staying awake all night to read and discuss the Torah and other holy works on Shavuot eve is called _____.

(a) *Tikkun Leyl Shavuot;* (b) *Gai Schluffen;* (c) *Ya'aleh V'yavo;* (d) *Leilah Tov.*

15. According to a folk tradition, why is it especially desirable to have good weather on Shavuot?

16. In Israel, to celebrate Shavuot, children have parades in which they carry baskets filled with what?

(a) Bibles; (b) nuts; (c) candy; (d) fruit.

17. On Shavuot, it is customary to eat what type of foods?

(a) meat dishes; (b) dairy dishes; (c) salty foods; (d) sour foods.

18. With what flowers was it customary to decorate synagogues and homes on Shavuot?

(a) lilacs; (b) gladiolas; (c) roses; (d) geraniums.

19. What's a *shevuosl?*

(a) a special Shavuot dessert; (b) a boy born on Shavuot; (c) a Shavuot decoration; (d) a Shavuot prayer.

20. True or false: Shavuot falls on a full-moon day.

**Shavuot:
Torah,
Torah, Torah**

Shavuot: Torah, Torah, Torah Answers

1. False. The Bible does not mention Shavuot in connection with the Torah. **2. (c)** Wednesday. (Shavuot occurs exactly seven weeks from the second day of Pesaḥ.) **3. (d)** David. (The holiday traditionally also marks the death of Abraham and the birth of Isaac.) **4.** Because the people of Israel had to purify themselves for three days in order to be ready to receive the Torah. **5. (b)** Mount Sinai (Exod. 19). **6. (a)** chapters in the Book of Psalms (said to be written by King David, who according to tradition was born and died on this holiday). **7. (a)** Mount Zion (because King David, who is said to have been born and died on the holiday, is buried there, according to tradition). **8. (d)** *Z'man Simḥatenu.* (This is another name for Sukkot.) **9.** True. *Megillat Ruth* is read on Shavuot. **10. (b)** study Hebrew. (Shavuot is considered an appropriate time because the Jews received the Torah on this day.) **11. (c)** the heavens open. **12. (d)** two loaves of bread (baked from the first product of the spring wheat harvest, for which thanksgiving is celebrated on Shavuot). **13. (c)** *Akdamut* (written by Rabbi Meir ben Isaac Nehorai of Worms, Germany, in the 12th century). **14. (a)** *Tikkun Leyl Shavuot.* (The custom was begun by 16th-century kabbalists in Safed.) **15.** Because if the weather is clear on Shavuot, there will be nice weather for the rest of the year. **16. (d)** fruit (because Shavuot is also known as the Festival of the First Fruits). **17. (b)** dairy dishes (because, according to one tradition, when they first received the Torah at Sinai and learned they were obligated to eat kosher meat, the Israelites realized that it would take time to prepare the meat, so they initially ate dairy. According to another tradition, it is because of the verse that compares the Torah to milk and honey.) **18. (c)** roses (because, according to one legend, Mount Sinai was covered with roses at the time the Torah was received). **19. (c)** a Shavuot decoration (an elaborate work of paper-cut art traditionally created to decorate the windowpanes of homes in Poland and Russia on Shavuot, also known as a *roysele*). **20.** False. It falls on the sixth day of the lunar month.

1. Young children just beginning their Hebrew lessons in a ḥeder traditionally studied which book of the Torah first?
(a) Genesis; (b) Exodus; (c) Leviticus; (d) Numbers.

2. In what year was the first Jewish ambassador to an Arab country appointed?
(a) 1979; (b) 1985; (c) 1990; (d) 1994.

3. According to Rava, a fourth-century Babylonian teacher, what is the first question God asks a person on Judgment Day?
(a) "Did you love your family?" (b) "Did you keep the mitzvot?" (c) "What do you have to say for yourself?" (d) "Were you reliable in your business dealings?"

4. Who are the *ḥaredi?*
(a) Israelis who emigrate; (b) ultra-Orthodox Jews; (c) soldiers in the Israeli army; (d) Israeli Arabs.

5. Which of the following refers to lifting up the Torah?
(a) *petiḥah;* (b) *hotza'ah;* (c) *gelilah;* (d) *hagbah;* (e) *hakhnasah.*

6. How many letters of the Hebrew alphabet take a special form at the end of words?
(a) three; (b) five; (c) seven; (d) nine.

Answers on page 126

7. Which tribe, because it refrained from worshiping the Golden Calf, was granted the privilege of performing the service in the sanctuary and, later, the Temple?
   (a) Levi;   **(b)** Judah;   **(c)** Benjamin;   **(d)** Naphtali.

8. The *hamsa* amulet, popular in eastern Jewish communities and believed to fend off the Evil Eye, is shaped like _____.
   (a) an eye;   **(b)** a foot;   **(c)** a hand;   **(d)** a Hebrew word.

9. *Get,* the name for a divorce decree, is an Aramaic word meaning _____.
   (a) "document";   **(b)** "divorce";   **(c)** "end";   **(d)** "agreement."

10. Who are the *Lamed-vavniks,* or "36ers"?

11. Which soldier—who later became a Zionist pioneer hero—was the only Jewish officer in the czar's army during the Russo-Japanese war of 1904?
   (a) David Ben-Gurion;   **(b)** Joseph Trumpeldor;   **(c)** Aaron David Gordon;
   (d) Vladimir Jabotinsky.

12. What is Miriam's well?

13. According to the Bible, what did manna taste like?
   (a) wafers in honey;   **(b)** roasted meat;   **(c)** milk and bread;   **(d)** sweet porridge.

14. True or false: The Talmud prohibits polygamy.

15. The curtain covering the Torah ark in many synagogues serves as a reminder of the curtain used in the Temple for what purpose?
(a) to separate the High Priest from the people; (b) to separate the Holy from the Holy of Holies; (c) to separate the men from the women; (d) to separate the area used for sacrifices from the rest of the Temple.

More for the Mavens

16. Boris Thomashefsky, Jacob Adler, and Zelig Mogulesco were _____.
(a) heroes of the American Revolution; (b) actors in the Yiddish theater; (c) early Reform rabbis; (d) founders of the Socialist party in the United States.

17. What kind of school did Albert Einstein attend as a child?
(a) a yeshivah; (b) a public school; (c) a Catholic school; (d) a prep school.

18. True or false: The Ku Klux Klan has always been an anti-Semitic organization.

19. What happened to French author Emile Zola after he wrote the newspaper article *"J'accuse,"* in which he declared that Jewish army captain Alfred Dreyfus, convicted of spying, had been framed?

(a) He died shortly afterward; (b) He was lauded as a national hero;
(c) He was convicted of libel and fled; (d) He became a lawyer and worked as a member of Dreyfus's defense team.

20. Who was Noa in the Bible?

Answers
126

More for the Mavens Answers

1. (c) Leviticus. (Leviticus Rabbah 7:3 points out that the young are pure, as are the offerings detailed in Leviticus: "Let the pure come to study the purities.") **2. (d)** 1994 (Marc Charles Ginsberg, U.S. ambassador to Morocco, appointed January 1994). **3. (d)** "Were you reliable in your business dealings?" **4. (b)** ultra-Orthodox Jews. (They live primarily in the Mea Shearim quarter of Jerusalem and in B'nei Brak, near Tel Aviv. The name means "fearful.") **5. (d)** *hagbah*. *Petiḥah* is the opening of the ark; *hotza'ah* is taking the Torah out; *gelilah* is tying it up; and *hakhnasah* is closing the ark. **6. (b)** five. **7. (a)** Levi. **8. (c)** a hand. (Both the hand and the number five are mentioned in numerous instances in the Torah and in Jewish legend; the five fingers of the hand were believed to protect against evil.) **9. (a)** "document." **10.** According to the Talmud, in every generation there are 36 righteous people who receive the Divine Presence; it is for their sake that God allows the world to continue. **11. (b)** Joseph Trumpeldor. **12.** A miraculous well of water flowing from a stone that accompanied the Israelites after the Exodus from Egypt, stopping when they camped and traveling as they wandered. It existed for nearly 40 years in the desert because of the righteousness of Miriam. **13. (a)** wafers in honey. **14.** False. Polygamy is permitted, though discouraged, in the Talmud. Rabbenu Gershom (960–1028) officially abolished it in the 10th century. **15. (b)** to separate the Holy from the Holy of Holies. **16. (b)** actors in the Yiddish theater. **17. (c)** a Catholic school. (His parents, assimilated German Jews, chose that form of education for him.) **18.** False. When first founded, the Klan focused its attention on carpetbaggers and accepted Jews and Catholics as members. **19. (c)** He was convicted of libel and fled (to England). **20.** Noa (נֹעָה) was a woman who, along with her sisters, Maḥla, Ḥagla, Milka, and Tirtza, asked Moses to allow them to inherit the estate of their father, Tzelafḥad (Num. 27). (The name of the man who built the ark is spelled נֹחַ.)

1. In what Hebrew year did Israel gain its independence?

2. What telephone number do Israelis dial for help in an emergency?
   (a) 911; (b) 111; (c) 101; (d) 411.

3. Who was the first European head of state to visit Israel?
   (a) Former British prime minister Margaret Thatcher; (b) Former French president François Mitterrand; (c) King Juan Carlos of Spain; (d) Former Polish president Lech Walesa.

4. Who was the second Arab leader to make a public visit to Israel?

5. Who was the first member of the British royal family to visit Israel?
   (a) Queen Elizabeth II; (b) Prince Philip; (c) Prince Charles;
   (d) Diana, Princess of Wales.

6. Where was former Israeli president Chaim Herzog born?
   (a) Israel; (b) Russia; (c) Ireland; (d) Poland.

7. What Jerusalem landmark was built by Suleiman the Magnificent under Turkish rule?
   (a) the walls of the Old City; (b) the Western Wall; (c) the Dome of the Rock mosque; (d) the Cardo.

Answers on page 134

8. The first forest planted in the land of Israel since the destruction of the Temple was established in 1904. After whom was it named?
(**a**) King David; (**b**) Maimonides; (**c**) Ahad Ha-Am; (**d**) Theodor Herzl.

9. In what year did the shekel replace the pound as the Israeli unit of currency?
(**a**) 1953; (**b**) 1978; (**c**) 1980; (**d**) 1985.

10. How long a term does the Israeli president serve?
(**a**) three years; (**b**) four years; (**c**) five years; (**d**) six years.

11. How long must a non-Jewish emigrant to Israel be a resident before he or she is eligible to apply for citizenship?
(**a**) one year; (**b**) three years; (**c**) five years; (**d**) ten years.

12. The picture that is stamped on the modern Israeli one-shekel coin is the same impression that was on the one-shekel coin in biblical times. What is the picture?
(**a**) three pomegranates; (**b**) a menorah; (**c**) a *Magen David;* (**d**) a hand.

13. Which of the following was *not* developed in Israel?
(**a**) the Merkava battle tank; (**b**) the Kfir C-22 fighter jet; (**c**) the Mirage fighter jet; (**d**) the Lavi jet fighter.

14. The Shrine of the Book, where the Dead Sea Scrolls are kept, is built on the grounds of which museum?

15. What city is known to Arabs as *al-Quds al-Sharif?*
    (a) Ramlah; (b) Nazareth; (c) Bethlehem; (d) Jerusalem.

16. In the biographies filled out by Knesset members before each session, how did Moshe Dayan list his occupation?
    (a) "soldier"; (b) "archaeologist"; (c) "writer"; (d) "farmer."

17. Which of the following people is buried at Bet She'arim?
    (a) Rabbi Judah ha-Nasi; (b) Golda Meir; (c) King David; (d) Martin Buber.

18. Kenyon Jerusalem, opened in 1994, is the city of Jerusalem's first _____.
    (a) shopping mall; (b) amusement park; (c) baseball-only stadium; (d) Reconstructionist congregation.

19. The first Israeli prime minister born in the Jewish state was _____.
    (a) David Ben-Gurion; (b) Moshe Sharett; (c) Levi Eshkol; (d) Yitzhak Rabin.

20. In what year did an Austrian head of state first visit Israel?
    (a) 1955; (b) 1968; (c) 1985; (d) 1994.

1. Which Jewish baseball player was the first American League MVP?
   (a) Ken Holtzman; (b) Steve Stone; (c) Al Rosen; (d) Ron Blomberg.

2. Who was the Jewish member of the 1995 Super Bowl champion San Francisco 49ers team?
   (a) Bart Oates; (b) Harris Barton; (c) Jay Fiedler; (d) Steve Young.

3. Harold Abrahams, a Jewish athlete from Britain, was the first European to win _____.
   (a) an Olympic sprint event; (b) the World Heavyweight Boxing title; (c) the PGA golf tournament; (d) the Indianapolis 500.

4. Which American League baseball player was proud of his nickname, SuperJew?
   (a) Al Rosen; (b) Hank Greenberg; (c) Ron Blomberg; (d) Mike Epstein.

5. Who was the second Jewish athlete to be elected to the Pro Football Hall of Fame?
   (a) Sid Luckman; (b) Ron Mix; (c) Benny Friedman; (d) Herschel Walker.

6. Which Jewish pitcher, as a rookie, beat Sandy Koufax for what would turn out to be Koufax's last regular-season defeat?

7. In what year was Israel first represented in the Winter Olympics?
   (a) 1952; (b) 1964; (c) 1976; (d) 1994.

Answers on page 134

8. In what year did Jewish pitching great Sandy Koufax pitch a perfect game?
(a) 1962; (b) 1963; (c) 1964; (d) 1965.

9. Name this Jewish basketball-playing father-and-son combination: The father, who played with the Syracuse Nationals of the NBA, was Rookie of the Year in 1949 and a 12-time All-Star and is in the Basketball Hall of Fame. His son played for the Utah Jazz, Denver Nuggets, Milwaukee Bucks, and Phoenix Suns.

10. Which Jew was the highest-paid professional baseball player for three years?
(a) Sandy Koufax; (b) Ken Holtzman; (c) Hank Greenberg; (d) Al Rosen.

11. Which Jewish athlete was the heroine of the U.S. women's gymnastics team at the 1996 Summer Olympics in Atlanta?
(a) Shannon Miller; (b) Kerri Strug; (c) Dominique Moceanu;
(d) Jaycie Phelps.

12. How many Jews played major-league baseball between 1871 and 1980?
(a) 42; (b) 115; (c) 235; (d) 427.

13. What did Jewish gymnasts Alfred and Gustav Flatow; fencers Oskar Gerde, Janos Garay, Attila Petchaur, and Endre Kabos; and boxer Victor Perez have in common?

(a) They all won Olympic gold medals; (b) They all became U.S. citizens and competed in the Olympics under the U.S. flag; (c) They all died in Nazi concentration camps; (d) They all were world-record holders.

14. The Jewish baseball player with the most hits racked up 2,131 in his career. Who is he?

(a) Al Rosen; (b) Hank Greenberg; (c) Buddy Myer; (d) Ron Blomberg.

15. In 1992, Israel won its first two Olympic medals in which sport?

(a) judo; (b) swimming; (c) track; (d) archery.

16. In 1938, when Hank Greenberg hit 58 home runs, he tied a record. What was the record?

17. Two American Jews, Marty Glickman and Sam Stoker, were scheduled to compete in the 400-meter relay in the 1936 Winter Olympics in Berlin but were replaced a few hours before the heats by two African-American runners, Ralph Metcalfe and _____.

18. The eligibility rules for Israel's Hapo'el games are different from those for the Maccabiah games. What's the difference?

19. Sandy Koufax, a Jew, was the youngest player ever to be elected to the Baseball Hall of Fame. How old was he?
　　(a) 29;　**(b)** 34;　**(c)** 37;　**(d)** 42.

20. Moe Berg, who had a 17-year career as a major-league catcher, was also _____.
　　(a) a lawyer;　**(b)** a linguist;　**(c)** a spy;　**(d)** all of these.

Holy Land, Modern Land Answers

1. 5708. **2. (c)** 101. **3. (b)** Former French president François Mitterrand (in 1983). **4.** King Hussein of Jordan, in November 1994. (The first Arab leader to openly visit Israel was President Anwar el-Sadat of Egypt.) **5. (b)** Prince Philip. (He went in October 1994 to visit Yad Vashem in Jerusalem and to receive a medal in honor of his mother, Princess Alice of Greece, who hid three Jews in her Athens home during the Nazi occupation.) **6. (c)** Ireland. **7. (a)** the walls of the Old City (1537–1540). **8. (d)** Theodor Herzl. **9. (c)** 1980. The rate was one shekel for every 10 pounds. **10. (c)** five years. **11. (b)** three years. **12. (a)** three pomegranates. **13. (c)** the Mirage fighter jet. (Israeli researchers at the Technion developed the Kfir C-22 after France prohibited delivery of its Mirage fighter jets to Israel.) **14.** The Israel Museum. **15. (d)** Jerusalem. (The name means "the holy and noble city.") **16. (d)** "farmer." **17. (a)** Rabbi Judah ha-Nasi. **18. (a)** shopping mall. **19. (d)** Yitzhak Rabin. **20. (d)** 1994. (Austrian president Thomas Klestil, in a speech before the Knesset, apologized for his country's role in the Holocaust.)

Athletes and All-Stars Answers

1. (c) Al Rosen (Cleveland Indians third baseman, 1947–56. He was MVP in 1953.) **2. (b)** Harris Barton (offensive tackle). **3. (a)** an Olympic sprint event (gold medal in 100-meter dash, 1924). **4. (d)** Mike Epstein. (He played nine years in the major leagues with Baltimore, 1966–67; Washington, 1967–71; Oakland, 1971–72; Texas, 1973; and California, 1973–74.) **5. (b)** Ron Mix. (The first was Sid Luckman.) **6.** Ken Holtzman. **7. (d)** 1994 (by a team consisting of one athlete, Misha Shmerkin, a figure skater who had emigrated to Israel from the Soviet Union in 1991). **8. (d)** 1965. (He pitched no-hitters in each of the other three years.) **9.** Dolph and Danny Schayes. **10. (c)** Hank Greenberg (1940, 1941, 1946). **11. (b)** Kerri Strug. **12. (b)** 115 (approximately 1 percent of the roughly 10,000 major-league ballplayers in that period). **13. (c)** They all died in Nazi concentration camps. **14. (c)** Buddy Myer. (Born Charles Solomon Myer, he played for 17 years, 15 of them with the Washington Senators.) **15. (a)** judo. Yael Arad and Oren Smadja won silver and bronze medals, respectively, in the 1992 games. **16.** Most home runs in a season for a right-handed hitter. (He tied with Jimmy Foxx.) **17.** Jesse Owens. (Glickman and Stoller were the only members of the U.S. track and field team who did not get a chance to compete in Berlin.) **18.** The Hapo'el games are open to everyone; the Maccabiah is limited to Jewish athletes. **19. (c)** 37 (1972). **20. (d)** all of these. (Berg studied law at Columbia University, spoke a dozen languages, and was an OSS operative during World War II.)

1. On which holiday, according to tradition, did manna begin to fall from heaven?
   (a) Sukkot; (b) Shavuot; (c) Lag B'Omer; (d) Tu B'Shevat.

2. On which minor festival did young women in ancient times dance before prospective suitors?
   (a) Tu B'Shevat; (b) Tu B'Av; (c) Lag B'Omer; (d) Hanukkah.

3. In Israel, Yom ha-Zikaron, or Remembrance Day, is observed on the day before which holiday?
   (a) Yom Kippur; (b) Pesaḥ; (c) Yom ha-Shoah; (d) Yom ha-Azma'ut.

4. Which holiday is sometimes known as the Scholars' Holiday?
   (a) Lag B'Omer; (b) Shavuot; (c) Purim; (d) Shemini Atzeret.

5. True or false: The holiday of Tu B'Shevat is mentioned in the Bible.

6. On which holiday is it customary in hasidic and other communities for people to offer prayers that God will help them find a beautiful *etrog* for Sukkot?
   (a) Yom Kippur; (b) Hanukkah; (c) Tu B'Shevat; (d) Lag B'Omer.

7. On Tu B'Shevat, it is customary to give a donation to charity totaling _____ dollars or cents.
   (a) 15; (b) 18; (c) 36; (d) 91.

Answers on page 142

8. In some traditions, it is customary to stay up late on the eve of Tu B'Shevat reciting passages of the Bible dealing with _____.

9. On Tu B'Shevat, it has been traditional among some Jews to eat a specified number of different fruits. How many?
(a) 4; (b) 15; (c) 18; (d) 91.

10. On Tu B'Shevat, some Jews eat jam made from a ritual object used on another holiday. What is it?

11. Some communities set up a *maot perot* fund to provide what for the poor on Tu B'Shevat?
(a) wheat; (b) clothes; (c) health care; (d) fruit.

12. The Israeli Knesset first proclaimed the observance of which holiday in 1951?
(a) Yom Yerushalayim; (b) Yom ha-Zikaron; (c) Yom ha-Azma'ut;
(d) Yom ha-Shoah.

13. Why has it become customary to light six *yahrzeit* candles on Yom ha-Shoah?

14. On the eve of Yom ha-Azma'ut, it is traditional for the speaker of the Knesset to light a torch on which Israeli mountain?
(a) Mount Herzl; (b) Mount Carmel; (c) Mount Moriah; (d) Mount Meron.

15. It is traditional for the official Israeli government commemoration of Yom ha-Azma'ut to include a gun salute. How many rounds are fired?
   (a) 5; **(b)** 21; **(c)** 48; **(d)** the number varies.

16. On which holiday is a televised Bible quiz held in Israel?
   (a) Shavuot; **(b)** Lag B'Omer; **(c)** Yom ha-Azma'ut; **(d)** Hanukkah.

17. What event is celebrated on Yom Yerushalayim?

18. On Lag B'Omer in Israel, a Torah scroll is carried in a procession from Safed to which village?
   (a) Modi'in; **(b)** Meron; **(c)** Tiberias; **(d)** Herzliah.

19. What happens during the Lag B'Omer ritual known as *opsherenish?*
   (a) Orthodox boys get their first haircut; **(b)** people stay up all night studying Torah; **(c)** an archery tournament is held; **(d)** a bonfire is lit.

20. Why is it traditional to celebrate Lag B'Omer with archery contests?

1. Which of the following symbols is *not* a recurrent motif in traditional Jewish art?
   (a) a pair of lions wearing crowns; **(b)** a pair of griffins wearing crowns;
   (c) an eagle; **(d)** a turkey.

2. Who created the menorah sculpture that stands in front of the Knesset building?
   (a) Yaacov Agam; **(b)** Jacques Lipchitz; **(c)** Benno Elkan; **(d)** Louise Nevelson.

3. Which Italian artist was born into a distinguished Jewish family from Livorno?
   (a) Modigliani; **(b)** Bernini; **(c)** Rafaello; **(d)** Donatello.

4. Which well-known artist became costume and stage designer for the newly established Kamerni Jewish State Theater in Moscow in 1920?
   (a) Marc Chagall; **(b)** Jacques Lipchitz; **(c)** Chaim Gross; **(d)** Ben Shahn.

5. What was the name of the colonial-era U.S. silversmith whose tureens, plates, and other works can be found in several American museums and who made Torah crowns for the first synagogues in Newport, R.I.; Philadelphia; and New York?
   (a) Levy Levy; **(b)** Sheftall Sheftall; **(c)** Phillip Phillips; **(d)** Myer Myers.

6. Which well-known New Jersey-born printmaker and sculptor, the son of a rabbi, attended an Orthodox yeshivah from age seven until age 14, when he decided to become an artist?
   (a) George Segal; **(b)** Leonard Baskin; **(c)** Max Weber; **(d)** Mark Rothko.

Answers on page 142

7. What was American surrealist artist Man Ray's original name?
(a) Emanuel Radnitsky; (b) Manny Rosenberg; (c) Manfred Mann;
(d) Myron Rapoport.

8. Israel's renowned school of arts and crafts, founded by Boris Schatz in 1906, is named after which biblical figure?
(a) Balaam; (b) Balak; (c) Bezalel; (d) Benjamin.

9. Which of the following is *not* a title of a work by Marc Chagall?
(a) *Time Is a River Without Banks;* (b) *Green Violinist;* (c) *White Crucifixion;* (d) *Flying Spice Box.*

10. Jewish artist Solomon Nunes Carvalho accompanied which explorer on his travels across the American West?
(a) La Salle; (b) Meriwether Lewis; (c) John C. Frémont; (d) Ponce de León.

11. Israeli artist Yaacov Agam, who developed "kinetic art," created all but one of the following works. Which one is not his?
(a) the rotating *Fire-Water Sculpture* in Tel Aviv's Dizengoff Square; (b) the façade of the Hotel Mondrian in Los Angeles; (c) the *Wings of the Heart* sculpture at New York's John F. Kennedy International Airport; (d) *Scroll of Fire,* a public monument near the village of Kesalon in the Judean hills commemorating the Holocaust and the rise of Israel.

12. Architect James Ingo Freed of Pei Cobb Freed and Partners (formerly I. M. Pei and Partners) designed which highly acclaimed building of Jewish interest?
(a) Yad Vashem; (b) the United States Holocaust Memorial Museum;
(c) the Shalom Tower; (d) Yad Kennedy.

13. Which famous synagogue has stained-glass windows created by Tiffany?
(a) Beth Sholom Congregation in Elkins Park, Pa.; (b) Temple Israel in Los Angeles; (c) Congregation Shearith Israel in New York City; (d) the Bevis Marks Synagogue in London.

14. Which historic synagogue was designed by Peter Harrison, the dean of American colonial architects, who also designed King's Chapel in Boston and Christ Church in Cambridge?
(a) Mikveh Israel in Philadelphia; (b) Shearith Israel in New York City;
(c) the Touro Synagogue in Newport, R.I.; (d) Rodeph Shalom in Philadelphia.

15. Why did Jewish jeans maker Levi Strauss put rivets on his pants?

16. Which world-class Israeli swimsuit company was founded by Leah Gottlieb?

17. Which fashion designer was the class clown at the Yeshivah of Flatbush and has received financial backing from the Sephardic Jewish community?
(a) Isaac Mizrahi; (b) Arnold Scaasi; (c) Ralph Lauren; (d) Calvin Klein.

18. Which fashion designer, the son of a furrier from Westmount, a well-to-do suburb of Montreal, changed his name by spelling it backward?

19. Judith Leiber, who began her handiwork because, as a Jew, she could not attend a university in her native Hungary in the 1930s and 1940s, is now world-famous as a designer of _____.
    (a) jewelry; **(b)** handbags; **(c)** shoes; **(d)** floral arrangements.

20. Which world-famous fashion designer, born Ralph Lifshitz, studied Hebrew and the Torah at Yeshiva University?

Holidays, Holidays, and More Holidays Answers

1. (c) Lag B'Omer. **2. (b)** Tu B'Av (the 15th of Av, the date that marriage was allowed between the different tribes of Israel). **3. (d)** Yom ha-Azma'ut. (Yom ha-Zikaron honors the memory of men and women who died in Israel's wars.) **4. (a)** Lag B'Omer (because a plague that struck the students of Rabbi Akiba suddenly stopped on that day). **5.** False. (It dates to talmudic times.) **6. (c)** Tu B'Shevat. (Sukkot, the harvest festival, is the culmination of how trees were judged on Tu B'Shevat.) **7. (d)** 91 (Because 91 is the numerical value of the letters in the Hebrew word *ilan* [tree]. Tu B'Shevat is the day of judgment for trees, and "charity averts the evil decree.") **8.** Trees, fruit, or the fertility of the earth (e.g., Gen. 1:11–13, Lev. 26:3–18, Deut. 8:1–10, Eze. 17, and Ps. 65:10–14). **9. (b)** 15 (perhaps as a celebration of the 15th of Shevat). **10.** *Etrog*s used on the previous Sukkot. **11. (d)** fruit. **12. (d)** Yom ha-Shoah. **13.** In memory of the 6 million Jews who were murdered in the Holocaust. **14. (a)** Mount Herzl (near the grave of Theodor Herzl). **15. (d)** the number varies (it corresponds to the year of independence). **16. (c)** Yom ha-Azma'ut. **17.** The reunification of the Old City with the rest of Jerusalem following 19 years of Arab rule. **18. (b)** Meron (the site of the graves of Rabbi Shimeon Bar Yohai and Rabbi Akiba, who were active in the revolt against the Romans that is commemorated on the holiday). **19. (a)** Orthodox boys get their first haircut. **20.** Because, according to legend, on that day Rabbi Akiba disobeyed the Roman government by taking his students into the wilderness to study Torah, carrying bows and arrows to make it seem as if they were going hunting.

Fashion, Art, and Architecture Answers

1. (d) a turkey. **2. (c)** Benno Elkan. **3. (a)** Modigliani. **4. (a)** Marc Chagall. **5. (d)** Myer Myers. **6. (b)** Leonard Baskin. **7. (a)** Emanuel Radnitsky. **8. (c)** Bezalel. (He built the Tabernacle in the wilderness—Exod. 31.) **9. (d)** *Flying Spice Box*. (This is a painting by Yosl Bergner.) **10. (c)** John C. Frémont. **11. (d)** *Scroll of Fire*. (This was created by Nathan Rappoport.) **12. (b)** the United States Holocaust Memorial Museum (Washington, D.C.). **13. (c)** Congregation Shearith Israel in New York City. **14. (c)** the Touro Synagogue in Newport, R.I. **15.** So that tools placed in the pockets would not rip them. **16.** Gottex. **17. (a)** Isaac Mizrahi. **18.** Arnold Scaasi (Isaacs). **19. (b)** handbags. **20.** Ralph Lauren.

1. Who wrote the poem beginning "My heart is in the East,/But I am in the utter-most West"?
   (a) Judah ha-Levi; (b) Ahad Ha-Am; (c) Allen Ginsberg; (d) Theodor Herzl.

2. The poet Rachel took care of which noted Israeli when he was a small child in Kibbutz Degania?
   (a) Menachem Begin; (b) Benjamin Netanyahu; (c) Moshe Dayan;
   (d) Shimon Peres.

3. Who wrote a poem called *In the Jewish Synagogue in Newport?*
   (a) Ralph Waldo Emerson; (b) Emma Lazarus; (c) Robert Browning;
   (d) William Wordsworth.

4. What was the pseudonym of Yiddish writer Shalom Jacob Abramowitsch?
   (a) Sholem Aleichem; (b) Yehoash; (c) Ahad Ha-Am; (d) Mendele Mocher Seforim.

5. I. L. Peretz, a major author in Yiddish and Hebrew, wrote his early works in which language?
   (a) English; (b) Ladino; (c) Polish; (d) Spanish.

Answers on page 151

6. In which language did Elie Wiesel write *Night, Dawn,* and most of his other works?
  (a) Yiddish; **(b)** French; **(c)** Polish; **(d)** English.

7. Who wrote the novel *Yekl?*
  (a) Abraham Cahan; **(b)** Isaac Bashevis Singer; **(c)** Sholem Aleichem;
  (d) Saul Bellow.

8. In the stage and film versions of *Fiddler on the Roof,* Tevye speaks of Jews' loyalty to "Tradition." What was the word in the original Yiddish story?

9. Henry Wadsworth Longfellow wrote a five-act play about which Jewish holiday?
  (a) Yom Kippur; **(b)** Sukkot; **(c)** Shavuot; **(d)** Hanukkah.

10. Which Jewish writer, who also won the Nobel Prize and the Pulitzer Prize, was the first American author to be awarded the French International Literature Prize?
  (a) Elie Wiesel; **(b)** Nelly Sachs; **(c)** Isaac Bashevis Singer; **(d)** Saul Bellow.

11. Which noted author wrote for the *Forward* under the name Isaac Warshofsky?

12. John Hersey's *The Wall* is the story of what event in Jewish history?
  (a) the defense of Masada; **(b)** the reunification of the Old City with the rest of Jerusalem; **(c)** the Warsaw Ghetto uprising; **(d)** the battle of Jericho.

13. Who was the first Hebrew writer to receive the Nobel Prize for literature?
   (a) I. L. Peretz; **(b)** S. Y. Agnon; **(c)** Yehuda Amichai; **(d)** Amos Oz.

14. Who were the children in the *All-of-a-Kind Family,* a popular young people's book series about Jewish life on the Lower East Side at the turn of the century?

15. How old was Pavel Friedmann, a prisoner in the concentration camp at Theresienstadt, when he wrote the poem *A Butterfly* in June 1942?
   (a) 6; **(b)** 11; **(c)** 15; **(d)** 20.

16. Which novelist, an observant Jew, wrote a guide to Judaism entitled *This Is My God?*
   (a) Saul Bellow; **(b)** Joseph Heller; **(c)** Herman Wouk; **(d)** Leon Uris.

17. Who wrote the novel on which the Steven Spielberg film *Schindler's List* was based?
   (a) Elie Wiesel; **(b)** Thomas Keneally; **(c)** Robert James Waller;
   (d) William Styron.

18. The name of which fictional character, created for a Jewish newspaper by Yiddish author Jacob Adler, has become a synonym in the Yiddish language for a gossip?

19. What was the pen name of 19th-century Zionist writer Asher Ginsberg?
   (a) Ahad Ha-Am; **(b)** Leo Pinsker; **(c)** Yehoash; **(d)** S. An-Ski.

20. Which female gentile author advocated the establishment of a Jewish homeland in Palestine?
   (a) Jane Austen; **(b)** Mary Shelley; **(c)** George Eliot; **(d)** Charlotte Brontë.

1. Who was the first person in the Bible to say a blessing?
   (a) Adam; (b) Eve; (c) Noah; (d) Abraham.

2. How long is the shortest prayer mentioned in the Bible?
   (a) two words; (b) four words; (c) five words; (d) six words.

3. True or false: The Bible commands Jews to pray three times a day.

4. Which time of day is considered inappropriate for prayer in Judaism?
   (a) between midnight and 2 A.M.; (b) the hour before sunrise; (c) after one has gotten into bed; (d) there is no inappropriate time for prayer.

5. True or false: Kneeling in prayer is against Jewish tradition.

6. True or false: The blessing recited before the reading of a Torah portion by the person honored with an *aliyah* is longer than the blessing recited after the reading.

7. True or false: The traditional prayers were written down and distributed among the public as soon as they were composed.

8. The last letters of the first and last words of the first sentence of the *Shema*, written large in the text of the Torah, form a word meaning _____.
   (a) "one"; (b) "hear"; (c) "witness"; (d) "God."

Answers on page 151

9. What holiday hymn was composed by a 13th-century liturgical poet named Mordecai whose name appears in an acrostic of the first letters of its five stanzas?

10. Which part of the Friday-evening liturgy is a poem written by kabbalist Solomon Alkabets?
(a) *Lekha Dodi;* (b) *Eshet Ḥayil;* (c) *Vayekhulu;* (d) *Shalom Aleikhem.*

11. Which hymn is a greeting to the two angels who, according to tradition, accompany Jews from the synagogue to their homes on Friday night?

12. Which part of the Friday-night ritual begins with the last two words of the first chapter of the Torah and immediately continues with the beginning of the second chapter?
(a) the *kiddush;* (b) the blessing over the candles; (c) *birkat hamazon;*
(d) *Eshet Ḥayil.*

13. According to third-century sages Rav and Rabbi Yohanan, what two attributes must a prayer have in order to be classified as a benediction?

14. When does one say the *ha-gomel* blessing?
(a) before eating a fruit for the first time in a season; (b) to give thanks for recovering from illness or escaping from danger; (c) upon seeing a rainbow;
(d) upon drinking liquor other than wine.

15. In traditional congregations, the response to the verse *Shema Yisra'el* is said under one's breath except _____.

    (a) on Shabbat; **(b)** on Rosh Hashanah; **(c)** on Yom Kippur;

    (d) there are no exceptions.

16. Which important part of the Jewish liturgy was originally used as a short prayer at the end of sermons given in Aramaic, about 2,000 years ago?

    (a) the *kiddush;* **(b)** the *Kaddish;* **(c)** the *Shema;* **(d)** *Ein Kelohenu.*

17. True or false: The mourner's *Kaddish* recited in a synagogue is the same as the *Kaddish* said at the cemetery after a burial.

18. The blessing, "Blessed are You, Lord our God, Ruler of the universe, whose strength and might fill the world" is said on all but one of the following occasions. On which occasion is this blessing not recited?

    (a) upon seeing a falling star; **(b)** upon experiencing an earthquake;

    (c) upon witnessing lightning and thunder; **(d)** upon seeing a rainbow.

19. How many stars must be visible in the sky before it is time to recite the *Maariv* service?

    (a) one; **(b)** two; **(c)** three; **(d)** five.

20. *Eshet Ḥayil,* recited by the father and children on Friday night in praise of the female head of the household and the feminine aspect of God, is composed of the last 22 verses of which book of the Bible?

(a) Proverbs; (b) Psalms; (c) Ruth; (d) Song of Songs.

People of the Book, Poem, and Story Answers

1. (a) Judah ha-Levi (1085–1142). 2. (c) Moshe Dayan. 3. (b) Emma Lazarus. (Henry Wadsworth Longfellow wrote a poem called *The Jewish Cemetery at Newport.*) 4. (d) Mendele Mocher Seforim. 5. (c) Polish. 6. (b) French. 7. (a) Abraham Cahan. 8. "Torah." 9. (d) Hanukkah *(Judas Maccabeus).* 10. (d) Saul Bellow. 11. Isaac Bashevis Singer. 12. (c) the Warsaw Ghetto uprising. 13. (b) S. Y. Agnon (1966). 14. Ella, Henrietta (Henny), Sarah, Charlotte, Gertie, and brother Charlie. 15. (b) 11. (He died in Auschwitz in 1944.) 16. (c) Herman Wouk. 17. (b) Thomas Keneally. 18. Yenteh Telebende. 19. (a) Ahad Ha-Am. 20. (c) George Eliot.

Prayers and Blessings Answers

1. (c) Noah (Gen. 9:26). 2. (c) five words. (When Moses asked God to heal his sister, Miriam, from leprosy, he said, "O God, please heal her"— *"Ayl na, refa na lah."*) 3. False. According to Maimonides, there is a biblical obligation to pray, but the number and form of the prayers were set later by the rabbis. 4. (d) there is no inappropriate time for prayer. 5. False. Kneeling was used in Temple times but has been limited to High Holy Days services in traditional congregations since the destruction of the Temple. 6. False. Each blessing consists of 20 words for a total of 40, which according to tradition alludes to the 40 days Moses spent on Mount Sinai. 7. False. Until the eighth century, tradition prohibited the writing down and publication of prayers. 8. (c) "witness." (Those who recite the *Shema* bear witness that God is One.) 9. "Maoz Tzur." 10. (a) *Lekha Dodi.* 11. *Shalom Aleichem.* 12. (a) the *kiddush.* 13. It must invoke the name of God and God's kingship. 14. (b) to give thanks for recovery from illness or escaping from danger. 15. (c) on Yom Kippur. (The response, which is not found in the Bible, is said under one's breath to distinguish it from the *Shema*'s biblical passages. On Yom Kippur it is said aloud to commemorate the Temple service, when the priests and people said it upon hearing the name of God pronounced by the High Priest.) 16. (b) the *Kaddish.* (The earliest allusion to it as a prayer for the dead occurs in *maḥzor* Vitry, dated 1208.) 17. False. An expanded version is recited at the cemetery. 18. (d) upon seeing a rainbow. On this occasion, one says: "Blessed are You, Lord our God, Ruler of the universe, who remembers the covenant [with Noah], who is trustworthy in His covenant and established in His word." 19. (c) three. 20. (a) Proverbs.

1. Tisha B'Av, the day of mourning for the Temple, is known as the "black fast." What's the "white fast"?

(a) the Fast of Tevet; (b) the 17th of Tammuz; (c) the Fast of Esther;
(d) Yom Kippur.

2. Which fast day is believed to be the day of the birth of the Messiah?

(a) Yom Kippur; (b) Tisha B'Av; (c) the Fast of Gedaliah; (d) the Fast of Tevet.

3. When is the proper time to bless the new moon in the months of Tishri and Av?

(a) before Yom Kippur/Tisha B'Av; (b) on Yom Kippur/Tisha B'Av; (c) after Yom Kippur/Tisha B'Av.

4. On which fast day has it become customary for Israelis to take hikes around the walls of the Old City of Jerusalem?

(a) Yom Kippur; (b) the Fast of Esther; (c) the Fast of the Firstborn;
(d) Tisha B'Av.

5. According to tradition, which fast day is the anniversary of the incident of the Golden Calf at Sinai?

(a) the 17th of Tammuz; (b) Tisha B'Av; (c) the Fast of Tevet; (d) the Fast of Gedaliah.

Answers on page 160

6. Which fast day, according to tradition, was designated by God as a day of mourning when the spies sent by Moses to Canaan came back with an unfavorable report?

(a) the Fast of Tevet; (b) the 17th of Tammuz; (c) Tisha B'Av; (d) the Fast of Gedaliah.

7. The *sefer kinot* is a booklet containing special prayers and readings for which fast day?

(a) Yom Kippur; (b) Tisha B'Av; (c) the Fast of Tevet; (d) the 17th of Tammuz.

8. True or false: The Fast of Gedaliah takes place on the day after Rosh Hashanah because Gedaliah was killed on that day.

9. Which fast day commemorates the beginning of Nebuchadnezzar's siege of Jerusalem?

(a) the 17th of Tammuz; (b) the Fast of Tevet; (c) Tisha B'Av; (d) the Fast of Gedaliah.

10. Members of a *ḥevrah kadishah* (burial society) traditionally fast on the seventh of Adar, to atone for any disrespect they may have shown to the dead. Why do they fast on this date?

(a) Because it falls one week before Purim, a merry holiday; (b) Because, according to tradition, the first funeral took place on this date; (c) Because it is the anniversary of the death of Moses; (d) Because it is commanded in the Torah.

11. In a family in which the firstborn child is a daughter and the second child a son, is the son obligated to fast on the Fast of the Firstborn, which takes place on the day before Pesaḥ?

12. How can a firstborn son become exempt from the Fast of the Firstborn preceding Pesaḥ?

(a) by convincing his parents to adopt an older son; (b) by donating the cost of three meals to charity; (c) by getting married on that date; (d) by attending a religious feast.

13. True or false: The fast of the 17th of Tammuz was instituted by the talmudic rabbis.

14. Which of the following activities is *not* prohibited during the three weeks of mourning between the 17th of Tammuz and the ninth of Av?

(a) getting a haircut; (b) getting engaged; (c) getting married; (d) buying a new home.

15. At the beginning of the month of Av, as a sign of mourning for the destruction of the Temple in anticipation of Tisha B'Av, it is traditional to abstain from consuming _____ and _____.

(a) meat and wine; (b) bread and water; (c) sugar and salt; (d) fruit and vegetables.

16. What is the last thing traditionally eaten before the Tisha B'Av fast?
(a) a piece of bread dipped in ashes; (b) a bitter herb dipped in ashes;
(c) a carrot dipped in ashes; (d) an egg dipped in ashes.

17. Which prophet is said to have written the Book of Lamentations, read on Tisha B'Av?
(a) Isaiah; (b) Jeremiah; (c) Ezekiel; (d) Jonah.

18. Why do women in some Sephardic and Eastern communities put on perfume on the afternoon of Tisha B'Av?

19. True or false: On Tisha B'Av the study of Torah is forbidden.

20. Why is it customary in some communities for Jews to leave their books of Tisha B'Av hymns behind when they leave services at the conclusion of the holiday?

1. The first public monument to the 6 million Jewish Holocaust victims in North America was dedicated in 1964 in which city?
   (a) Philadelphia; (b) New York; (c) Toronto; (d) Miami Beach.

2. The first museum memorializing those killed in the Holocaust was built in which country?
   (a) Israel; (b) Russia; (c) the United States; (d) France.

3. The first printing press in Palestine was established in which city in the 16th century?
   (a) Jerusalem; (b) Safed; (c) Beersheba; (d) Lydda.

4. Which country borders Israel on the northeast?
   (a) Lebanon; (b) Jordan; (c) Syria; (d) Egypt.

5. Which modern country was the Babylonia of biblical and talmudic times?
   (a) Iran; (b) Iraq; (c) Syria; (d) Saudi Arabia.

6. The Tigris-Euphrates river valley, at the head of the Persian Gulf, is believed to be which biblical site?
   (a) the Garden of Eden; (b) Sodom and Gomorrah; (c) Canaan; (d) Ur.

Answers on page 160

7. Where was the birthplace of Haym Salomon, Jewish hero of the American Revolution?

(a) Philadelphia; (b) England; (c) Poland; (d) Russia.

8. What was the first U.S. municipality to be named after a Jew?

(a) Cohens Bluff, S.C.; (b) Mendes, Ga.; (c) Levittown, Pa.; (d) Aaronsburg, Pa.

9. In the early 20th century, Maxwell Street was the center of the Eastern European Jewish community in which U.S. city?

(a) New York; (b) Philadelphia; (c) Chicago; (d) Detroit.

10. The stretch of 15th Street, S.W., just south of Independence Avenue in Washington, D.C., where the United States Holocaust Memorial Museum is located, was renamed in honor of whom?

(a) Mordecai Anilewicz; (b) Raoul Wallenberg; (c) Anne Frank;
(d) Oskar Schindler.

11. Which one of the following U.S. states has no town, county, or other geographical unit named after a Jew?

(a) Colorado; (b) New Mexico; (c) Maryland; (d) Arkansas.

12. The first rabbinical school in America was located in which city?

(a) Cincinnati; (b) New York; (c) Los Angeles; (d) Philadelphia.

13. Among numerous charitable contributions, Jewish civic leader and philanthropist Judah Touro established the Touro Free Library, reputedly the first free public library in the world, in 1824. Where was it located?

(a) New Orleans; (b) Newport, R. I.; (c) New York City; (d) Charleston, S.C.

14. Uriah P. Levy, a Jewish hero of the U.S. Navy who served in the War of 1812, bought and restored which national landmark?

(a) the Liberty Bell; (b) the Washington Monument; (c) Monticello;
(d) the Betsy Ross house.

15. In which city is the oldest Jewish cemetery in the United States located?

(a) Newport, R.I.; (b) Philadelphia; (c) New York; (d) Richmond, Va.

16. Which city was nicknamed "the Jerusalem of Poland" because it was a center of Torah study from the 16th to the 18th centuries?

(a) Warsaw; (b) Krakow; (c) Lublin; (d) Lodz.

17. The first Jewish quarter in Europe was located in _____.

(a) Venice; (b) Rome; (c) Trieste; (d) Modena.

18. The Rue des Rosiers was the Jewish section in which city?

(a) Montreal; (b) Brussels; (c) Geneva; (d) Paris.

19. The oldest Jewish community in Europe is located in which city?
   (a) London; **(b)** Rome; **(c)** Paris; **(d)** Prague.

20. November 29 Street in Jerusalem *(Reḥov Kaf-Tet b'November)* was named in commemoration of the date of _____.
   (a) the United Nations vote granting the Jews a homeland; **(b)** Theodor Herzl's birthday; **(c)** the issuance of the Balfour Declaration; **(d)** the signing of the Israel-Egypt peace treaty.

Where in the World . . . ?

A Time for Fasting Answers

1. (d) Yom Kippur. (It is known as the "white fast" because it is the most holy day of the year.) **2. (b)** Tisha B'Av. **3. (c)** after Yom Kippur/Tisha B'Av. At a time of atonement or mourning, one cannot be in a joyous mood, which is proper for blessing the moon. **4. (d)** Tisha B'Av. **5. (a)** the 17th of Tammuz. **6. (c)** Tisha B'Av. **7. (b)** Tisha B'Av. **8.** False. Gedaliah, the governor of Judah, was murdered on Rosh Hashanah, but it is prohibited to fast on the New Year festival. The fast is therefore postponed until the day after (except when that day falls on Shabbat, in which case the fast is postponed until Sunday). **9. (b)** the Fast of Tevet. **10. (c)** Because it is the anniversary of the death of Moses. **11.** No. (Since the firstborn child is a daughter, the son is not firstborn.) **12. (d)** by attending a religious feast (such as the one that takes place upon completion of study of a tractate of the Talmud). **13.** False. Like Tisha B'Av, the fast of the 17th of Tammuz predates the Talmud. **14. (b)** getting engaged (although engagement parties are prohibited). Growing one's hair was an ancient sign of mourning. Weddings are forbidden because their joy conflicts with mourning for the Temple, although engagements are permitted for fear that they would be broken if postponed. Buying a new home or doing anything requiring recitation of the *she-he-ḥeyanu* is prohibited during the mourning period. **15. (a)** meat and wine. **16. (d)** an egg dipped in ashes. **17. (b)** Jeremiah. **18.** To welcome the Messiah, who, according to tradition, will be born on Tisha B'Av. **19.** True. Torah study, because it is a source of spiritual pleasure, is prohibited on Tisha B'Av. (It is also prohibited during *shivah.*) **20.** The custom expresses their belief that before the next Tisha B'Av the Messiah will come and the day will be turned into a festival.

Where in the World . . . ? Answers

1. (a) Philadelphia (the Monument to the Six Million Jewish Martyrs). **2. (d)** France. (Ground was broken in 1946 for the Mémorial du Martyr Juif Inconnu in Paris.) **3. (b)** Safed. **4. (c)** Syria. **5. (b)** Iraq. **6. (a)** the Garden of Eden. **7. (c)** Poland. **8. (d)** Aaronsburg, Pa. (It was founded in 1786 by Aaron Levy.) **9. (c)** Chicago. **10. (b)** Raoul Wallenberg (the Swedish businessman and diplomat who helped save about 100,000 Hungarian Jews from the Nazis in 1944). **11. (c)** Maryland. **12. (d)** Philadelphia. (Maimonides College, founded 1867. It closed after six years owing to a lack of national support.) **13. (a)** New Orleans. **14. (c)** Monticello. **15. (a)** Newport, R.I. **16. (c)** Lublin. **17. (a)** Venice (in 1516). It was located next to a cannon factory, or *giotto* in Italian, which reportedly was the origin of the word "ghetto." **18. (d)** Paris. **19. (b)** Rome. (It dates to at least 180 B.C.E.) **20. (a)** the United Nations vote granting the Jews a homeland (Nov. 29, 1947).

1. Which musical group in the 1960s recorded a song based on the third chapter of Ecclesiastes?

(a) the Byrds; (b) Peter, Paul, and Mary; (c) Crosby, Stills, and Nash;
(d) the Beach Boys.

2. Which Yiddish folk song tells of a *rebbe* sitting near the fireplace teaching his class to read Hebrew?

(a) "Bei Mir Bistu Shein"; (b) "Oyfin Pripehchick"; (c) "Rozhinkes Mit Mandlen"; (d) "A Brivele Der Mamen."

3. Why did the late Cantor Samuel Arluck of Temple Adath Yeshurun in Syracuse, N.Y., weave the tune "Over the Rainbow" into his services?

(a) Because MGM studio head Louis B. Mayer was a congregant; (b) Because he originally was from Kansas; (c) Because his son wrote the song;
(d) Because the Torah portion for the day was Genesis 9, in which Noah sees the rainbow.

4. The song "Kaḥol ve-Lavan" ("Blue and White"), about the Israeli flag, was first heard in which country?

(a) Israel; (b) the Soviet Union; (c) the United States; (d) Canada.

5. Palestine colonist Samuel Cohen wrote the music for which anthem?

6. In Temple times, only *kohanim* were permitted to play which musical instrument?

    (a) the harp; **(b)** the drum; **(c)** the flute; **(d)** the trumpet.

7. What song was written by Rabbi Shlomo Carlebach in response to a 1965 request by Glen Richter and Yaakov Birnbaum, leaders of the Student Struggle for Soviet Jewry, to compose a song for the Soviet Jewry movement?

    (a) "Maḥar"; **(b)** "Bashana Haba'a"; **(c)** "Am Yisra'el Ḥai"; **(d)** "Kuma Ekha."

8. A Hebrew phrase that today constitutes the lyrics to a well-known song was used as a code to pass the message that it was time to celebrate Rosh Ḥodesh after the Roman conquest of Israel, when it was forbidden to practice Judaism. What is the phrase?

9. Which of the following songs was written by Israeli composer-singer Naomi Shemer?

    (a) "Hai, Ḥai, Ḥai"; **(b)** "Shir Hashalom"; **(c)** "Erev Shel Shoshanim";
    (d) "Yerushalayim Shel Zahav."

10. Which atonal composer, who fled the Nazis and came to the United States in 1933, wrote the opera *Moses and Aaron* as well as the pieces *Kol Nidre* and *A Survivor from Warsaw?*

    (a) Arnold Schoenberg; **(b)** Anton Weber; **(c)** Alban Berg; **(d)** Igor Stravinsky.

11. Which hit song, first performed in 1969, was released in English in the United States under the title "Any Time of the Year"?
(a) "Maḥar"; (b) "Bashana Haba'a"; (c) "Erev Shel Shoshanim"; (d) "Bei Mir Bistu Shein."

12. The Boston-based Hawthorne String Quartet has recorded and performed the work of Jewish composers Pavel Haas, Gideon Klein, Hans Krasa, and Viktor Ullmann. What do these composers have in common?
(a) They were imprisoned in the concentration camp at Terezin; (b) They all won Grammy awards; (c) They were former cantors; (d) They all immigrated to Israel from Europe.

13. Why did radio stations in Palestine during the British Mandate repeatedly play parts of the "Moldau" composition by Bedrich Smetana?

14. Which song, introduced at the first Israel Hasidic Song Festival in 1969, takes its lyrics from a line in the *Kaddish?*

15. In the Yiddish song "Tumbalalaika," whose lyrics are in the form of a riddle, what grows without rain, what yearns without tears, and what can burn forever?

16. The sixth movement of Beethoven's C-Sharp Minor String Quartet contains a musical theme that is very similar to the melody of _____.
  (a) the *Kol Nidre;* **(b)** *Ein Kelohenu;* **(c)** "Hatikvah"; **(d)** *Yigdal.*

17. The Israeli song "Hamilḥama Ha-aḥrona" ("The Last War") was released during which war?
  (a) the War of Independence; **(b)** the Six-Day War; **(c)** the Yom Kippur War;
  (d) the Persian Gulf War.

18. Where was Zubin Mehta, music director of Israel's national orchestra, born?
  (a) Palestine; **(b)** India; **(c)** Argentina; **(d)** Pakistan.

19. In what year did the Israel Philharmonic make its first tour of the United States?
  (a) 1949; **(b)** 1951; **(c)** 1957; **(d)** 1968.

20. The first professional cantorial school in the United States was located _____.
  (a) at the Jewish Theological Seminary; **(b)** at Yeshiva University;
  (c) at Hebrew Union College–Jewish Institute of Religion; **(d)** at Brandeis University.

1. Early Russian Zionists in the period before Theodor Herzl's activism in the late 1890s were known as _____.
    (a) Ḥovevei Zion; (b) Poalei Zion; (c) Gush Emunim; (d) Va'ad Leumi.

2. What is the oldest Jewish national fraternal order in the United States?
    (a) B'nai B'rith; (b) the Free Sons of Israel; (c) the American Jewish Congress;
    (d) the Zionist Organization of America.

3. What was the first separate U.S. charitable institution serving the Jewish community specifically?
    (a) B'nai B'rith; (b) ORT; (c) the Female Hebrew Benevolent Society;
    (d) the Hebrew Immigrant Aid Society (HIAS).

4. What was the only pre-Holocaust Jewish scholarly institution to escape annihilation by the Nazis by moving its mission and materials to America?
    (a) ORT; (b) the Alliance Israélite Universelle; (c) YIVO Institute for Jewish Research; (d) the Workmen's Circle.

5. 18 Mila St. was the address of which organization?

Answers on page 169

6. Which Jewish group places a classified ad on the front page of each Friday's *New York Times* announcing the time that Shabbat candles should be lit?
(a) B'nai B'rith; (b) Agudath Israel; (c) the Lubavitcher hasidim; (d) the Council of Jewish Federations.

7. Which Jewish organization, which was in the planning stages in 1915, was established ahead of schedule after the lynching of Jewish pencil-factory worker Leo Frank in Georgia?
(a) the American Jewish Committee; (b) the American Jewish Congress;
(c) the Jewish Defense League; (d) the Anti-Defamation League of B'nai B'rith.

8. Who founded the World Zionist Organization?
(a) Henrietta Szold; (b) Theodor Herzl; (c) David Ben-Gurion; (d) Golda Meir.

9. The Arbeiter Ring, a Jewish organization of workers, is known by what name in English?
(a) the Labor Zionist Alliance; (b) United Jewish Appeal; (c) the Workmen's Circle; (d) Jewish Community Center.

10. True or false: The Jewish War Veterans group is older than the American Legion, the Veterans of Foreign Wars, and the Disabled American Veterans.

11. In 1933–34, Golda Meir served as general secretary of which American Jewish women's organization?

    (a) Hadassah; **(b)** Women's League for Conservative Judaism;

    (c) Pioneer Women; **(d)** Women's American ORT.

12. The Bundes Brueder was the original name for which organization, founded by 12 German Jews in New York in 1843?

13. Which worldwide Orthodox organization sponsors the Beth Jacob School system for girls?

    (a) Agudath Israel; **(b)** the Lubavitcher hasidim; **(c)** Mizraḥi Women;

    (d) the Satmar hasidim.

14. Which Jewish organization publishes *Commentary* magazine?

    (a) the American Jewish Congress; **(b)** the American Jewish Committee;

    (c) the National Jewish Community Relations Advisory Council;

    (d) the American Jewish Historical Society.

15. Which pogrom—the largest in history—inspired American Jews to respond by founding the United Jewish Appeal?

16. Which youth movement is sponsored by Hadassah, the Women's Zionist Organization of America?
(a) Ha-Shomer Ha-Tza'ir; (b) Young Israel Youth; (c) United Synagogue Youth; (d) Young Judaea.

17. What is the more well-known name of the Yidisher Visnshaftlekher Institut?

18. Which American Jewish woman founded the Hebrew Sunday School Society in 1838?
(a) Henrietta Szold; (b) Emma Lazarus; (c) Rebecca Gratz;
(d) Hannah Greenebaum Solomon.

19. What was the first national Jewish women's organization in the United States?
(a) Hadassah; (b) Pioneer Women; (c) the National Council of Jewish Women;
(d) B'nai B'rith Women.

20. The first nationwide gathering of U.S. Jewish religious leaders occurred in 1859 under the auspices of which Jewish organization?
(a) the Synagogue Council; (b) the United Synagogue of America;
(c) the Board of Rabbis; (d) the Board of Delegates of the American Israelites.

Musical Matters Answers

1. (a) the Byrds ("Turn, Turn, Turn"). **2. (b)** "Oyfin Pripehchick." **3. (c)** Because his son (composer Harold Arlen) wrote the song. **4. (b)** the Soviet Union. (The melody is Russian.) **5.** "Hatikvah." **6. (d)** the trumpet. **7. (c)** "Am Yisra'el Ḥai." **8.** *David melekh Yisra'el ḥai ve-kayam."* **9. (d)** "Yerushalayim Shel Zahav" ("Jerusalem of Gold"). **10. (a)** Arnold Schoenberg. **11. (b)** "Bashana Haba'a." **12. (a)** They were imprisoned in the concentration camp at Terezin. (They kept composing and performing during their incarceration.) **13.** Because the piece was said to be the inspiration for the melody of "Hatikvah," which was banned from public air waves by the British during the Mandate. **14.** "Oseh Shalom." **15.** A stone can grow without rain, a heart can yearn without tears, and love can burn forever. **16. (a)** the *Kol Nidre.* **17. (c)** the Yom Kippur War. **18. (b)** India. **19. (b)** 1951. **20. (c)** at Hebrew Union College–Jewish Institute of Religion (its School of Sacred Music in New York, established in 1948).

The Organized Jewish Community Answers

1. (a) Ḥovevei Zion ("Lovers of Zion"). **2. (b)** the Free Sons of Israel (established in 1849). **3. (c)** the Female Hebrew Benevolent Society (founded by several women from Congregation Mikveh Israel in Philadelphia, including Rebecca Gratz, in 1825). **4. (c)** YIVO Institute for Jewish Research. **5.** The Zydowska Organizacja Bojowa (Jewish Fighting Organization), the Jewish underground in the Warsaw Ghetto, headed by Mordecai Anielewicz. **6. (c)** the Lubavitcher hasidim. **7. (d)** the Anti-Defamation League of B'nai B'rith. **8. (b)** Theodor Herzl. **9. (c)** the Workmen's Circle. **10.** True. The Jewish War Veterans (founded as the Hebrew Union Veterans Organization, adopting its current name in 1929), was established in 1896 as an organization of Civil War veterans. The American Legion was founded in 1919, the Veterans of Foreign Wars in 1913, and the Disabled American Veterans in 1935. **11. (c)** Pioneer Women (now known as Na'amat). **12.** B'nai B'rith. **13. (a)** Agudath Israel. **14. (b)** the American Jewish Committee. **15.** Kristallnacht. **16. (d)** Young Judaea. **17.** YIVO Institute for Jewish Research. **18. (c)** Rebecca Gratz. **19. (c)** the National Council of Jewish Women (founded in 1893). **20. (d)** the Board of Delegates of the American Israelites.

1. The Sabbath is described as a bride in the hymn *Lekha Dodi*. Who or what is the bridegroom?

(a) God; (b) the work week; (c) the people Israel; (d) Moses.

2. *Benchn licht* on Shabbat is a Yiddish phrase referring to what practice?
(a) saying the grace after meals; (b) saying a blessing over the candles;
(c) saying the *kiddush;* (d) saying the parents' blessing for their children.

3. True or false: The Bible commands Jews to light the Shabbat lights.

4. On Shabbat evening, it is customary for parents to bless their children. Girls are encouraged to be like the matriarchs Sarah, Rebecca, Rachel, and Leah. Boys are encouraged to be like Ephraim and Menashe, who were _____.
(a) the sons of Joseph; (b) the sons of Jacob; (c) the sons of Moses; (d) the sons of Noah.

5. According to tradition, Jews who are careful to eat the three Shabbat meals will be saved from what fate?
(a) going hungry; (b) not having a place in the World to Come; (c) suffering indigestion; (d) getting caught up in the war between Gog and Magog against Israel.

6. True or false: El Al airplanes do not fly on Shabbat.

Answers on page 174

7. Why are the 18 benedictions of the weekday *Amidah* reduced to seven on Shabbat?

8. According to the Talmud, who ordained that the Torah be read on Shabbat?
   (a) Ezra; **(b)** Aaron; **(c)** Abraham; **(d)** Moses.

9. What direction does the congregation in European and North American synagogues face while chanting the last stanza of *Lekha Dodi?*
   (a) north; **(b)** east; **(c)** west; **(d)** south.

10. According to the Talmud, the practice of reading the haftarah on Shabbat goes back to _____.
   (a) the first century B.C.E.; **(b)** the first century C.E.; **(c)** the fifth century C.E.;
   (d) the 12th century C.E.

11. If you forget to light candles on a particular Shabbat, what does the Shulḥan Arukh say you should do?
   (a) bless the ḥallah; **(b)** forgo Shabbat observance that week; **(c)** fast;
   (d) add another candle permanently from then on.

12. What is the name given to objects that, because they are used for work, are forbidden to be handled on Shabbat?
   (a) *muktsa;* **(b)** *trefe;* **(c)** *derekh eretz;* **(d)** *demai.*

13. According to tradition, King David was told by God that he would die on Shabbat. What did he do each Shabbat day to prevent the Angel of Death from having power over him?

(a) He hid; (b) He spent the day studying Torah; (c) He wore a disguise;
(d) He went to a mikveh.

14. What is Shabbat Mevarḥim?

(a) the Shabbat preceding Tisha B'Av; (b) the Shabbat following Tisha B'Av;
(c) the Shabbat preceding the new moon; (d) the Shabbat when the Song of Moses is read in the synagogue.

15. Which Shabbat commemorates the yearly gift to the treasury for Temple sacrifices?

(a) Shabbat Zakhor; (b) Shabbat Parah; (c) Shabbat Shekalim;
(d) Shabbat Naḥamu.

16. What is the name of the special Shabbat at which the sermon traditionally includes an explanation of the laws relating to *hametz,* the story of the Exodus from Egypt, or the text of the haggadah?

(a) Shabbat Shuvah; (b) Shabbat Ḥazon; (c) Shabbat Shirah;
(d) Shabbat ha-Gadol.

17. After Shabbat has ended, it is customary to have a special fourth meal known as a _____.

    (a) *melaveh malkah;* **(b)** *seudat shelishit;* **(c)** *oneg shabbat;* **(d)** *b'tayavon.*

18. True or false: According to Jewish law, wine or grape juice must be used for *havdalah.*

19. Why is a braided candle used for the *havdalah* ritual?

20. According to legend, why should a young man or woman hold the *havdalah* candle up high?

Sabbath Joy Answers

1. (c) the people Israel. **2. (b)** saying a blessing over the candles. **3.** False. There is no biblical commandment concerning Shabbat lights. According to Mishnah Shabbat 2:6, Shabbat candlelighting has been practiced since ancient times. The blessing is not quoted in the Talmud but is found in the ninth-century *siddur* of Rav Amram Gaon. **4. (a)** the sons of Joseph. (They carried on the life of the Jewish people.) **5. (d)** getting caught up in the war between Gog and Magog against Israel. (The war will precede the coming of the Messiah.) **6.** True. **7.** Because the Talmud prohibits petitions for help on Shabbat, so as not to disturb the atmosphere of the day. **8. (d)** Moses. **9. (c)** west. (The congregation, which normally faces east toward Jerusalem in European and North American synagogues, turns to the back of the room to face west while chanting the last stanza, in order "to greet the Sabbath bride.") **10. (b)** the first century C.E. **11. (d)** add another candle permanently from then on. **12. (a)** *muktsa*. (Observant Jews refrain from handling on the Sabbath anything pertaining to work, lest they forget the holiness of the day. The word means "set aside" or "stored away.") **13. (b)** He spent the day studying Torah. (He died on Shavuot, which fell on a Saturday, after the Angel of Death distracted him from his studies.) **14. (c)** the Shabbat preceding the new moon. (On this Shabbat the coming new month is announced, and a prayer is said that the month be one of health, prosperity, and fulfillment.) **15. (c)** Shabbat Shekalim. **16. (d)** Shabbat ha-Gadol (the Shabbat preceding Pesaḥ). **17. (a)** *melaveh malkah* ("escorting of the Queen"). **18.** False. Any beverage other than water may be used. **19.** Because the blessing over the light says, "Creator of the lights of fire," the rabbinical authorities ruled that there must be at least two candles with two wicks, which led to the evolution of a braided candle. **20.** So he or she will find a tall bride or groom.

Answers
174

1. When Theodor Herzl died, who replaced him as head of the World Zionist Organization?
   (a) David Ben-Gurion; (b) Chaim Weizmann; (c) Vladimir Jabotinsky; (d) Aaron David Gordon.

2. How many times did Albert Einstein visit Jerusalem?
   (a) never; (b) once; (c) twice; (d) five times.

3. What was the last name of the pioneering Hebrew poet who was popularly known simply as Rachel?
   (a) Blaustein; (b) Deganiah; (c) Eytan; (d) Yannait.

4. Which of the following is *not* true of psychotherapist and media personality Dr. Ruth Westheimer?
   (a) She was raised in an Orthodox Jewish home; (b) She escaped the Nazis in Germany by taking refuge in a Swiss orphanage; (c) She joined the Haganah in Palestine; (d) She has had only one husband.

5. Which renowned Jewish philosopher nearly converted to Christianity, but decided against it after observing what he intended to be his last Yom Kippur?
   (a) Martin Buber; (b) Abraham Joshua Heschel; (c) Franz Rosenzweig; (d) Walter Benjamin.

Answers on page 183

6. How many years did Teddy Kollek serve as mayor of Jerusalem?
(a) 12; (b) 17; (c) 28; (d) 35.

7. Which Israeli hero lost his left arm in combat?
(a) Moshe Dayan; (b) Yonatan Netanyahu; (c) Reuven Sadeh;
(d) Joseph Trumpeldor.

8. Which former Israeli president was the son of a chief rabbi?

9. How many years did Norman Podhoretz serve as editor-in-chief of the Jewish monthly *Commentary?*
(a) 15; (b) 25; (c) 35; (d) 40.

10. To whom was the Balfour Declaration, promising the formation of modern Israel, addressed?
(a) Lord Lionel Rothschild; (b) Baron Edmond de Rothschild; (c) Prime Minister David Lloyd George; (d) Chaim Weizmann; (e) David Ben-Gurion.

11. What is the name of the German Zionist woman who, in the early 1930s, sent Jewish children to Palestine to escape the Nazis in a program that was to become known as Youth Aliyah?
(a) Haviva Reich; (b) Hannah Senesh; (c) Rachel Cohen; (d) Recha Freier.

12. True or false: Albert Einstein was awarded the Nobel Prize for developing the theory of relativity.

13. Which 19th-century American Jewish activist was known as "Queen of the Platforms" for her advocacy of the abolitionist and women's rights movements?
    (a) Sophie Loeb; **(b)** Penina Moise; **(c)** Adah Isaacs Menken;
    (d) Ernestine Rose.

14. Which famed Israeli archaeologist discovered two mikvehs, a synagogue, and 25 skeletons on Masada?

15. Gluckel of Hameln, a German Jewish woman who lived in the 18th century, achieved a place in history for _____.
    (a) being the first woman *Rosh Yeshivah;* **(b)** keeping a Yiddish diary that provided a historical record of the Jewish community; **(c)** her brave resistance to a pogrom; **(d)** raising a generation of talmudic scholars.

16. What happened to Alfred Dreyfus, the Jewish French army captain wrongfully convicted of spying, whose case inspired Theodor Herzl to take up the Zionist cause?
    (a) He died in prison on Devil's Island; **(b)** After his release from Devil's Island, he emigrated to Palestine; **(c)** After his release from Devil's Island, he was reinstated in the French army; **(d)** After his release from Devil's Island, he emigrated to the United States.

17. The initial meeting of Palestine's first organized self-defense group, Hashomer, was held in 1907 in the one-room apartment of a man who later became president of Israel. Who was it?

(a) Chaim Weizmann; (b) Yitzhak Ben-Zvi; (c) Zalman Shazar;
(d) Ephraim Katzir.

18. Who was Moshe Pearlstein?

(a) the first American to die in Israel's War of Independence; (b) the first president of Yeshiva University's Albert Einstein College of Medicine;
(c) the first surgeon general of the Israeli army; (d) a Brooklyn-born biochemist who won the Nobel Prize in 1977.

19. Which Russian writer was a *shabbos goy*—a gentile employed to do things that Jews are forbidden to do on the Sabbath—as a young man?

(a) Alexander Solzhenitzyn; (b) Boris Pasternak; (c) Maxim Gorky;
(d) Feodor Dostoevsky.

20. True or false: Theodor Herzl's articles about a Jewish state were published in the *Neue Freie Presse*, the newspaper for which he worked.

1. Who was the first U.S. president to appoint a Jew to his Cabinet?
   (a) Andrew Jackson; (b) Millard Fillmore; (c) Theodore Roosevelt;
   (d) Franklin Roosevelt.

2. What was the first U.S. war in which rabbis were appointed as Army chaplains?
   (a) the Spanish-American War; (b) the Civil War; (c) World War I;
   (d) World War II.

3. Which U.S. presidential campaign was the first in which more Jews voted Democratic than Republican?
   (a) Harry S. Truman vs. Thomas E. Dewey; (b) Franklin D. Roosevelt vs. Herbert Hoover; (c) Adlai E. Stevenson vs. Dwight D. Eisenhower;
   (d) Alfred E. Smith vs. Herbert Hoover.

4. The first American Jew to be appointed to a high diplomatic post was Mordecai Manuel Noah, named consul to Tunis. Which president appointed him?
   (a) George Washington; (b) Thomas Jefferson; (c) James Madison;
   (d) Martin Van Buren.

5. Which hero of the American Revolution was known as the "Jewish Paul Revere" because of his ability to inspire the colonists to action?
   (a) Haym Salomon; (b) Uriah P. Levy; (c) Francis Salvador;
   (d) Sheftall Sheftall.

6. Jewish Supreme Court Justice Felix Frankfurter's best students from Harvard University, whom he brought to Washington, D.C., to run the New Deal, were known as his _____.

(a) Happy Hot Dogs; (b) Boys' Club; (c) Ivy Legion; (d) Crimson Crew.

7. Which first lady, in a famous incident, resigned from New York's Colony Club to protest the snubbing of a Jewish woman by its membership?

(a) Barbara Bush; (b) Hillary Rodham Clinton; (c) Eleanor Roosevelt;
(d) Betty Ford.

8. Which of the following Jews was not a vocal advocate for the abolition of slavery?

(a) Rabbi David Einhorn; (b) Rabbi Morris J. Raphall; (c) August Bondi;
(d) Michael Helprin.

9. Where was Jewish Supreme Court Justice Louis Brandeis born?

(a) Louisville, Ky.; (b) Boston; (c) Kiev; (d) New York City.

10. Ruth Bader Ginsburg and Stephen Breyer, two Jews, are serving simultaneously on the U.S. Supreme Court. Which two previous Jewish justices served on the Court simultaneously?

11. True or false: An Orthodox Jew has never served in the U.S. Senate.

12. In January 1995, the Jerusalem public square at Jabotinsky, Shalom Aleichem, and Yitzhak Elchanan Streets was renamed to honor which deceased U.S. senator?
    (a) Henry Jackson; **(b)** Jacob Javits; **(c)** Robert Kennedy; **(d)** John Heinz.

13. What happened to Judah Benjamin, the Jewish secretary of state of the Confederacy, after the Civil War?

14. Which U.S. president signed legislation establishing the United States Holocaust Memorial Council and mandating it to construct the United States Holocaust Memorial Museum?
    (a) Harry S. Truman; **(b)** John F. Kennedy; **(c)** Jimmy Carter;
    (d) Ronald Reagan.

15. What was President Franklin D. Roosevelt's nickname for Jewish Supreme Court Justice Louis Brandeis?
    (a) "Isaiah"; **(b)** "my rabbi"; **(c)** "Solomon"; **(d)** "Buddy."

16. Which U.S. general called upon his troops to emulate the "great army" of the "Children of Israel"?
    (a) George Washington; **(b)** Dwight D. Eisenhower; **(c)** Colin Powell;
    (d) Norman Schwartzkopf.

17. The first official Jewish delegation to call on the White House came to visit which president?

(a) John Quincy Adams; (b) James Polk; (c) James Buchanan;
(d) Grover Cleveland.

18. Meyer London of New York's Lower East Side was for many years the only _____ in the U.S. Congress.

(a) Jew; (b) hasidic Jew; (c) Socialist; (d) naturalized citizen.

19. The first serious attempt by a Jew to run for the U.S. presidency occurred in which election year?

(a) 1960; (b) 1968; (c) 1976; (d) 1996.

20. Which U.S. president moved his official residence to the home of Jewish citizen Isaac Franks to reduce the chance of taking ill during a yellow fever epidemic?

(a) George Washington; (b) John Adams; (c) Thomas Jefferson;
(d) James Madison.

Movers, Shakers, and Stars Answers

1. **(b)** Chaim Weizmann. 2. **(b)** once (in 1923). 3. **(a)** Blaustein. 4. **(d)** She has had only one husband. 5. **(c)** Franz Rosenzweig. 6. **(c)** 28. 7. **(d)** Joseph Trumpeldor. 8. Chaim Herzog. (His father was Isaac Herzog, who was chief rabbi of the Irish Free State in 1921 and became chief rabbi of Palestine in 1937.) 9. **(c)** 35. 10. **(a)** Lord Lionel Rothschild. 11. **(d)** Recha Freier. 12. False. Einstein received the Nobel in 1921 for his discovery of the law of the photoelectric effect. 13. **(d)** Ernestine Rose. 14. Yigael Yadin. 15. **(b)** keeping a Yiddish diary that provided a historical record of the Jewish community. 16. **(c)** After his release from Devil's Island, he was reinstated in the French army. 17. **(b)** Yitzhak Ben-Zvi (president from 1953 to 1963). 18. **(a)** the first American to die in Israel's War of Independence. 19. **(c)** Maxim Gorky. 20. False. Although Herzl worked for the *Neue Freie Presse,* the paper refused to publish his articles about a Jewish state. They were published in a pamphlet entitled *The Jewish State: An Attempt at a Modern Solution of the Jewish Question.*

America: The *Goldene Medina* Answers

1. **(c)** Theodore Roosevelt. (The Cabinet member was Oscar Straus, secretary of commerce and labor.) 2. **(b)** the Civil War. (A special decree from President Abraham Lincoln was required.) 3. **(d)** Alfred E. Smith vs. Herbert Hoover (1928 campaign). 4. **(c)** James Madison (in 1813). 5. **(c)** Francis Salvador. (He was also the first Jew to die fighting for the American Revolution, in July 1776.) 6. **(a)** Happy Hot Dogs. 7. **(c)** Eleanor Roosevelt. (The Jewish woman was Elinor Morgenthau, the wife of Henry Morgenthau, Jr.) 8. **(b)** Rabbi Morris J. Raphall. 9. **(a)** Louisville, Ky. 10. Louis Brandeis (1916–39) and Benjamin Cardozo (1932–38). 11. False (Sen. Joseph Lieberman, a Democrat from Connecticut). 12. **(a)** Henry Jackson. 13. Pursued by Union troops, he hid in the homes of Confederate sympathizers until he was safely able to board a boat to Cuba. From there, he went to England, where he became a leading member of the bar. 14. **(c)** Jimmy Carter (Public Law 96-388, Oct. 7, 1980). 15. **(a)** "Isaiah" (because of the biblical prophet's emphasis on justice). 16. **(a)** George Washington (in a broadside issued to the Continental Army in 1777 while it was encamped at Peekskill, N.Y.). 17. **(c)** James Buchanan. (They were protesting a commercial treaty with Switzerland that discriminated against American Jews doing business there.) 18. **(c)** Socialist. (He served in 1915–19 and 1921–23). 19. **(c)** 1976 (by Pennsylvania governor Milton Shapp, who sought the Democratic nomination). 20. **(a)** George Washington. (Franks lived in the Germantown section of Philadelphia.)

1. Which rabbi was the editor of the Mishnah?
   (a) Rabbi Judah ha-Levi; (b) Rabbi Judah ha-Nasi; (c) Rabbi Hillel;
   (d) Rabbi Akiba.

2. Who was known as "the Jewish Aristotle" because of his philosophical writings and his efforts to reconcile Aristotelian philosophy with Judaism?
   (a) Maimonides; (b) Nachmanides; (c) Gersonides; (d) Rabbenu Tam.

3. Beruriah, the woman whose learning and intellect are described in several stories in the Talmud, and for whom a women's seminary in Jerusalem is named, was the wife of which rabbi?
   (a) Rabban Gamaliel; (b) Rabbenu Tam; (c) Rabbi Meir; (d) Rashi.

4. Saadiah, Judah ha-Levi, and Maimonides wrote their philosophical works in which language?
   (a) Hebrew; (b) Aramaic; (c) Yiddish; (d) Arabic.

5. Who was the *Besht?*

6. What was the name of the wife of Rabbi Akiba, who married him despite the disapproval of her wealthy father, encouraged him to study Torah, and sold her hair to support his studies?
   (a) Rachel; (b) Rebecca; (c) Judith; (d) Deborah.

Answers on page 192

7. Maimonides wrote the first comprehensive code of Jewish law, called the *Mishneh Torah.* What does the title mean?

8. What is the name of the commentary on the Pentateuch written by Ishmael ben Elisha?
(a) Shulḥan Arukh; (b) *Sefer Ha-Mitzvot;* (c) *Mekhilta;* (d) *Pirke Avot.*

9. Third-century Palestinian *amora* (interpreter of the Oral Law) Rabbi Simeon ben Lakish was commonly known by what name?

10. Israel ben Eliezer was the founder of which movement?
(a) Hasidism; (b) the Enlightenment; (c) the kabbalists; (d) the Essenes.

11. Which 12th-century scholar became a physician to earn a living because he felt it was a sin "to utilize the words of the Torah as a spade with which to dig" (*Pirke Avot* 4:5)?
(a) Nachmanides; (b) Maimonides; (c) Rashi; (d) Rabbenu Tam.

12. The work *Ḥafetz Ḥaim*—which became so highly respected that its author, Rabbi Israel Meir Kagan (1838–1933), was always referred to as "the *Ḥafetz Ḥaim*—is a legal code enumerating all the earlier teachings on what topic?
(a) kashrut; (b) marriage and divorce; (c) the holidays; (d) slander.

13. Which rabbi was known as the Rashbi?
    (a) Rabbi Shlomo ben Isaac; (b) Rabbi Simeon bar Yohai; (c) Rabbi Shabbetai ben Meir ha-Kohen; (d) Rabbi Asher ben Israel.

14. Which 16th-century rabbi was known as ha-Ari (The Lion)?
    (a) Rabbi David ben Samuel ha-Levi; (b) Rabbi Joseph Karo; (c) Rabbi Moses Isserles; (d) Rabbi Isaac Luria.

15. Twelfth-century Rabbi Jacob ben Meir of Troyes, France, is also known as _____.

    (a) Ralbag; (b) the Rav; (c) Rabbenu Tam; (d) Radbaz.

16. What is Rabbi Hillel II credited with formulating in 359 C.E.?
    (a) the Jewish calendar; (b) the Shabbat worship service; (c) the Passover seder; (d) the Jewish marriage ceremony.

17. The Sanhedrin, or Jewish Supreme Court, was led for 10 generations by the descendants of which rabbi?
    (a) Rashi; (b) Rabbi Yohanan ben Zakkai; (c) Rabbi Judah ha-Nasi; (d) Rabban Gamaliel.

18. Which philosopher and halakhic authority wrote the *Book of Beliefs and Opinions*, the first major work of Jewish philosophy in the Middle Ages?

    (a) Rabbi Isaac Alfasi; **(b)** Saadiah Gaon; **(c)** Gersonides; **(d)** Rabbenu Tam.

19. True or false: Maimonides practiced astrology.

20. The book of Jewish mysticism called the Zohar cites a talmudic rabbi as its author. Which rabbi?

    (a) Rabbi Meir; **(b)** Rabbi Tarfon; **(c)** Rabbi Eliezer; **(d)** Rabbi Simeon bar Yohai.

1. The Great, the Hambro, and the New are names of the three _____.
   (a) kosher restaurants on Hester Street on New York's Lower East Side;
   (b) nightclubs on Dizengoff Street in Tel Aviv; (c) original Ashkenazic synagogues in London; (d) first Jewish-owned dry-goods stores in Chicago.

2. What day of the week is considered especially lucky for Jews?
   (a) Sunday; (b) Tuesday; (c) Thursday; (d) Friday.

3. The Wishnatzki & Nathel company of Plant City, Fla., which distributes produce to supermarkets, uses which Jewish symbol on its labels?
   (a) a *Magen David;* (b) a menorah; (c) a *dreidel;* (d) an image of the Israeli flag.

4. What Yiddish word takes its name from Shlumeayl, leader of the tribe of
   Shimon in biblical times?

5. True or false: A hairdresser and manicurist may work in a mikveh.

6. What is the name of the biblical beast that in one day eats the pastures on a
   thousand hills and can drink all the water that flows from the Jordan River into
   the sea in one gulp?
   (a) leviathan; (b) behemoth; (c) ziz; (d) barnacle goose.

Answers on page 192

7. What did Theodor Herzl wear to the First Zionist Congress in Basel, Switzerland, in 1897?

(a) a military uniform; (b) a disguise, for fear of being arrested; (c) full morning dress and a top hat; (d) a *tallit* and kippah.

8. In what year was Coca-Cola first exported to Israel?

(a) 1949; (b) 1955; (c) 1968; (d) 1972.

9. El Al's first commercial flights, in August 1949, served which two European cities?

(a) London and Zurich; (b) London and Brussels; (c) Vienna and Paris;
(d) Rome and Paris.

10. A band popular on the Jewish-music circuit is Benny and the _____.

(a) Boychiks; (b) Vildachayas; (c) Menschen; (d) Jets.

11. According to a folk belief, what will happen to a woman who sees a horse upon leaving the mikveh?

(a) She will go on a journey; (b) She will conceive a happy child that night;
(c) She will become ill; (d) She will have good luck.

12. What is the name of Yeshiva University's basketball team?

13. Which Israeli martial art takes its name from the Hebrew words "contact combat"?

14. True or false: According to Jewish law, it is permissible to use soaps made from pig fat, wear pigskin suede, and play football with a ball made from pigskin.

15. People with the last name Schatz probably had ancestors who performed which function in the synagogue?
(a) caretaker; (b) treasurer; (c) prayer leader; (d) congregational president.

16. Which of the following is *not* the name of a head covering for Orthodox women?
(a) *shaytl;* (b) *tichel;* (c) *gartel;* (d) *shterntichel.*

17. In what year was the first International Yiddish Festival held?
(a) 1927; (b) 1945; (c) 1976; (d) 1990.

18. What was the name of the *Jewish Daily Forward*'s famous advice column, which featured responses to readers' letters?

19. Honi ha-M'agel (Honi the Circle-Maker) was the _____ of the Talmud.
(a) Rip Van Winkle; (b) Ebenezer Scrooge; (c) Forrest Gump;
(d) Sherlock Holmes.

20. What is Israel's leading export industry?
   (a) the fruit and produce industry; **(b)** the electronics industry;
   (c) the diamond industry; **(d)** the textile industry.

Scholars and Sages Answers

1. (b) Rabbi Judah ha-Nasi (135–220 C.E.). **2. (a)** Maimonides. **3. (c)** Rabbi Meir (second century). **4. (d)** Arabic.
5. Israel *Baal Shem Tov*, the founder of Hasidism. **6. (a)** Rachel. **7.** "A second Torah." **8. (c)** *Mekhilta*. **9.** Resh Lakish. **10. (a)** Hasidism (Israel ben Eliezer is also known as Israel Baal Shem Tov.) **11. (b)** Maimonides.
12. (d) slander. **13. (b)** Rabbi Simeon bar Yohai. (The anniversary of his death is celebrated on Lag B'Omer.)
14. (d) Rabbi Isaac Luria. **15. (c)** Rabbenu Tam. **16. (a)** the Jewish calendar. **17. (d)** Rabban Gamaliel.
18. (b) Saadiah Gaon (882–942). **19.** False. In a letter responding to a question from the rabbis of southern France, he wrote that, according to the Torah, people's fate is determined by God and not by the stars. (At the time, however, very few Jewish scholars agreed with him.) **20. (d)** Rabbi Simeon bar Yohai. (According to many scholars, however, the Zohar was actually written 12 centuries after his death.)

Answers
192

Just for Fun Answers

1. (c) original Ashkenazic synagogues in London. **2. (b)** Tuesday. (Of the seven days of creation, the third day, or Tuesday, is the only one about which the Bible mentions twice that God saw that it was good.)
3. (a) a *Magen David.* **4.** *Schlemiel.* When the tribes of Israel went to war, Shimon—led by Shlumeayl, the first *schlemiel*—always suffered the greatest losses in battle, even when Israel emerged victorious. **5.** True. In fact, many mikvehs have them. **6. (b)** behemoth. **7. (c)** full morning dress and a top hat. **8. (c)** 1968.
9. (d) Rome and Paris. **10. (b)** Vildachayas. **11. (b)** She will conceive a happy child that night. (If she sees a dog, she will have an ugly child; if she sees an ass, the child will be stupid.) **12.** The Maccabees. **13.** *Krav maga* (invented by Imi Lictenfeld, a Czech who emigrated to Palestine to escape the Nazis and joined the Israeli army in 1948). **14.** True. Although pigs are not kosher to eat, it is permissible to benefit from a pig in other ways. **15. (c)** prayer leader. The name is an abbreviation for *shaliaḥ tzibur,* or prayer leader. **16. (c)** *gartel* (belt). A *shaytl* is a wig; a *tichel* is a scarf; a *shterntichel* is a cap and scarf that also covers part of the forehead. **17. (d)** 1990 (in Krakow, Poland). **18.** *A Bintel Brief* ("A Bundle of Letters"). **19. (a)** Rip Van Winkle. (Honi, according to *Ta'anit* 23a, saw a man planting a carob tree, fell asleep, and awoke 70 years later to see the man's grandson gathering fruit from the tree.) **20. (c)** the diamond industry.

Books

Angel, Marc D. *The Rhythms of Jewish Living: A Sephardic Approach.* Brooklyn, N.Y.: Sepher-Hermon Press, 1986.

Ben-Asher, Naomi, and Hayim Leaf, eds. *The Junior Jewish Encyclopedia,* 9th rev. ed. New York: Shengold Publishers, 1979.

Besser, James David. *Do They Keep Kosher on Mars?* New York: Collier Books, 1990.

Birnbaum, Philip. *A Book of Jewish Concepts.* New York: Hebrew Publishing Co., 1964.

Bloch, Abraham P. *The Biblical and Historical Background of Jewish Customs and Ceremonies.* New York: Ktav Publishing House, 1980.

Brownstone, David M. *America's Ethnic Heritage Series: The Jewish-American Heritage.* New York: Facts on File Publications, 1988.

Bulka, Reuven P. *What You Thought You Knew About Judaism.* Northvale, N.J.: Jason Aronson, 1989.

Burstein, Chaya M. *A Kid's Catalog of Israel.* Philadelphia: Jewish Publication Society, 1988.

Butwin, Frances. *The Jews in America.* Minneapolis: Lerner Publications, 1969.

Cardozo, Arlene Rossen. *Jewish Family Celebrations.* New York: St. Martin's Press, 1982.

Chafets, Ze'ev. *Heroes and Hustlers, Hard Hats and Holy Men: Inside the New Israel.* New York: William Morrow & Co., 1986.

Chetkin, Len. *Guess Who's Jewish?* Norfolk, Va.: The Donning Co., 1985.

Cohen, Sarah Blacher, ed. *From Hester Street to Hollywood.* Bloomington: Indiana University Press, 1983.

Davis, Sammy, Jr., and Jane and Burt Boyar. *Yes I Can.* New York: Farrar, Straus, & Giroux, 1965.

Dayan, Moshe. *Living with the Bible.* New York: William Morrow & Co., 1978.

Dershowitz, Alan M. *Chutzpah.* Boston: Little, Brown & Co., 1991.

Diamant, Anita, and Howard Cooper. *Living a Jewish Life.* New York: HarperCollins, 1991.

Eidlitz, E. *Is It Kosher? Encyclopedia of Kosher Foods Facts and Fallacies.* Jerusalem: Feldheim Publishers, 1992.

Eisenberg, Azriel. *The Synagogue Through the Ages.* New York: Bloch Publishing Co., 1974.

Epstein, Morris. *All About Jewish Holidays and Customs,* rev. ed. New York: Ktav Publishing House, 1970.

Fine, Leon. *Will the Real Israel Please Stand Up?* Kiron: Pelmas/Massada Ltd., 1983.

Ganzfried, Solomon, tr. Hyman Z. Goldin. *Code of Jewish Law (Kitzur Shulhan Aruh).* New York: Hebrew Publishing Co., 1961.

Gaster, Theodor H. *Festivals of the Jewish Year,* 1st paperback ed. New York: Morrow Quill Paperbacks, 1978.

Geffen, Rela M., ed. *Celebration and Renewal: Rites of Passage in Judaism.* Philadelphia: Jewish Publication Society, 1993.

Goldberg, J.J. *The Jewish Americans.* New York: Mallard Press, 1992.

Goldberg, M. Hirsh. *Just Because They're Jewish.* New York: Stein and Day Publishers, 1979.

Goldstein, David. *Jewish Legends.* New York: Peter Bedrick Books, 1987.

Golomb, Morris. *Know Jewish Living and Enjoy It.* New York: Shengold Publishers, 1981.

Greenberg, Irving. *The Jewish Way: Living the Holidays.* New York: Summit Books, 1988.

Greenberg, Judith E., and Helen H. Carey. *Jewish Holidays: A First Book.* New York: Franklin Watts, 1984.

Gross, David C. *The Jewish People's Almanac,* rev. ed. New York: Hippocrene Books, 1994.

The Guinness Book of Records, Bantam ed. New York: Bantam Books, 1994.

Gutstein, Linda. *History of the Jews in America.* Secaucus, N.J.: Chartwell Books, 1988.

Hausdorff, David M. *A Book of Jewish Curiosities.* New York: Crown Publishers, 1955.

Isaacs, Stephen D. *Jews and American Politics.* Garden City, N.Y.: Doubleday & Co., 1974.

Jacobs, Louis. *What Does Judaism Say About...?* New York: Quadrangle/The New York Times Book Co., 1973.

The Jewish People: A Pictorial History. Jerusalem: Keter Publishing House, 1974.

Kampf, Avram. *Jewish Experience in the Art of the Twentieth Century.* South Hadley, Mass.: Bergin & Garvey Publishers, 1984.

Kernfeld, Barry, ed. *The New Grove Dictionary of Jazz,* vol. 1. London: Macmillan Press Ltd., 1988.

Kolatch, Alfred J. *Who's Who in the Talmud.* New York: Jonathan David Publishers, 1964.

Kozodoy, Ruth. *The Book of Jewish Holidays.* New York, Behrman House, 1981.

Latner, Helen. *The Book of Modern Jewish Etiquette.* New York: Schocken Books, 1981.

Levine, Peter. *Ellis Island to Ebbets Field: Sport and the American Jewish Experience.* New York: Oxford University Press, 1992.

Library of Nations: Israel. Amsterdam: Time-Life Books, 1986.

Lutske, Harvey. *The Book of Jewish Customs.* Northvale, N.J.: Jason Aronson, 1986.

Lyman, Darryl. *Great Jews in Music.* Middle Village, N.Y.: Jonathan David Publishers, 1986.

Lyons, Len, and Don Perlo. *Jazz Portraits: The Lives and Music of the Jazz Masters.* New York: William Morrow & Co., 1989.

Maltin, Leonard. *Leonard Maltin's 1996 Movie and Video Guide.* New York: Penguin Books, 1995.

Markowitz, Endel. *The Encyclopedia Yiddishanica.* Fredericksburg, Va.: Haymark Publications, 1980.

Meyer, Michael A. *Hebrew Union College–Jewish Institute of Religion: A Centennial History, 1875–1975,* rev. ed. Cincinnati: Hebrew Union College Press, 1992.

Morgenstern, Dan. *Jazz People.* New York: Harry N. Abrams, 1976.

Morton, Frederic. *The Rothschilds: A Family Portrait.* New York: Atheneum, 1962.

The New Encyclopaedia Britannica, 15th ed. Chicago: Encyclopaedia Britannica, 1985.

Postal, Bernard, and Lionel Koppman. *A Jewish Tourist's Guide to the U.S.* Philadelphia: Jewish Publication Society, 1954.

Press, Chaim. *What Is the Reason,* vol. 1 (Rosh Hashanah). Brooklyn, N.Y.: Balshon Printing and Offset Co., 1964.

Renberg, Dalia Hardof. *The Complete Family Guide to Jewish Holidays.* New York: Adama Books, 1985.

Roth, Cecil. *The Jewish Book of Days,* rev. ed. New York: Hermon Press, 1968.

Schauss, Hayyim. *The Jewish Festivals: History and Observance.* New York: Schocken Books, 1975.

Schoener, Allon. *The American Jewish Album: 1654 to the Present.* New York: Rizzoli, 1983.

Shamir, Ilana, Shlomo Shavit, et al., eds. *Encyclopedia of Jewish History.* New York: Facts on File Publications, 1986.

Sharansky, Natan. *Fear No Evil.* New York: Random House, 1988.

Siegel, Richard, and Carl Rheins, eds. *The Jewish Almanac.* New York: Bantam Books, 1980.

Silverman, Buddy Robert S. *The Jewish Athletes' Hall of Fame.* New York: Shapolsky Publishers, 1989.

Simonhoff, Harry. J*ewish Notables in America from 1776 to 1865.* New York: Greenberg: Publisher, 1956.

Spitz, Leon. *The Bible, Jews and Judaism in American Poetry.* New York: Behrman's Jewish Book Shop, 1923.

Strassfeld, Michael. *The Jewish Holidays: A Guide and Commentary.* New York: Harper & Row Publishers, 1985.

Syme, Daniel B. *The Jewish Home: A Guide for Jewish Living.* New York: UAHC Press, 1988.

Taylor, Sidney. *All-of-a-Kind Family.* New York: Dell Publishing Co., 1951.

Telushkin, Joseph. *Jewish Literacy.* New York: William Morrow & Co., 1991.

Unterman, Alan. *Dictionary of Jewish Lore and Legend.* London: Thames and Hudson Ltd., 1991.

Waskow, Arthur. *Seasons of Our Joy.* Boston: Beacon Press, 1982.

Wasson, Tyler, ed. *Nobel Prize Winners.* New York: H.W. Wilson Co., 1987.

Westheimer, Ruth, with Ben Yagoda. *All in a Lifetime.* New York: Warner Books, 1987.

Who's Who in Israel, 1990–91, 21st biennial English ed. Tel Aviv: Who's Who in Israel Publishers Ltd., 1991.

Wigoder, Geoffrey. *Dictionary of Jewish Biography.* New York: Simon & Schuster, 1991.

Wigoder, Geoffrey, ed. *The Encyclopedia of Judaism.* New York: Macmillan Publishing Co., 1989.

Articles

Abraham, Henry J., "The heirs of King Solomon," *Jewish Exponent,* Dec. 9, 1994, page 14–X.

Alpert, Carl, "Is Israel running out of hope for 'Hatikvah'?" *Jewish Exponent,* April 14, 1995, page 25.

Anderson, A. Engler, "Focus: Magical, mystical holiday: On Lag B'Omer, paying homage to a holy one," *Jewish Exponent,* May 12, 1995, page 3.

Applebaum, Elizabeth, "Tell me why," *Palm Beach Jewish Times,* Feb. 3, 1995, page 10.

Applebaum, Elizabeth, "Tell me why: What's in a name?" *Palm Beach Jewish Times,* March 10, 1995, page 13.

Applebaum, Elizabeth, "Tell me why: Do you know-a Noa?" *Palm Beach Jewish Times,* March 3, 1995, page 13.

Bar, Naama, "Out on a limb," *JNF Illustrated,* Spring 1994, pages 16–19.

"Bar Ilan U names Barasch Florida campaign director," *Palm Beach Jewish Journal North,* Jan. 24–30, 1995, page 9A.

"Beer-Sheva is home to Ben-Gurion University," *Palm Beach Jewish Journal Israeli Independence Day Supplement,* May 2–8, 1995, page 12.

Bertugli, David, "From bags to riches," *Inside,* 10(3):21, Fall 1989.

Besser, James D. "Arlen Specter aims for the top," *Jewish Exponent,* March 31, 1995, pages 30–32.

Bloom, Cecil, "Beethoven's Jewish connection," *Jewish Quarterly,* 38(1):26–28, Spring 1991.

Blum, Debra E. "Connecticut's Israel network," *Chronicle of Higher Education,* Feb. 3, 1995, page A43.

Brown, Leon, " 'American synagogue' shows the Wright stuff," *Jewish Exponent,* Oct. 28, 1994, page 15.

Carpey, Sissy, "Stumbling on history," *Jewish Exponent,* April 28, 1995, page 1-X.

Chabin, Michele, "The Americanization of Israel," *Inside,* 16(2):36, Summer 1995.

Dershowitz, Alan, "Rosh Hashanah 'davening' with President Clinton," *Jewish Exponent,* Sept. 16, 1994, page 11.

"Diamonds are one of Israel's leading exports," *Palm Beach Jewish Journal Israeli Independence Day Supplement,* May 2–8, 1995, page 20.

Dinur, Yitzchak, "Keeping an eye on Einstein," *Scopus: Magazine of the Hebrew University of Jerusalem,* 43:30–32, 1993/94.

"Eilat is Israel winter resort with beaches, casinos," *Palm Beach Jewish Journal Israeli Independence Day Supplement,* May 2–8, 1995, page 11.

Elkin, Michael, "On the scene: Four questions for creator of 'Rugrats,' " *Jewish Exponent,* April 14, 1995, page 5-X.

Elkin, Michael, "Showcase says…'Picket Fences' opens a gate of stardom for Fyvush," *Jewish Exponent,* Sept. 23, 1994, page 5-X.

Freedman, Chaim, "Prenumeranten as a source for Jewish genealogists," *Avotaynu,* 10(2):42–45, Summer 1994.

Friedman, Sally, "Questions abound when first seder is on Saturday," *Jewish Exponent*, March 18, 1994, page 6.

Ghazali, Said, "Jordan's Hussein in Israel," *Philadelphia Inquirer*, Nov. 11, 1994, page A3.

Gilson, Estelle, "YIVO—Where Yiddish scholarship lives," *Present Tense*, 4:57-65, Autumn 1976.

Goldberger, Paul, "Passions set in stone," *New York Times Magazine*, Sept. 10, 1995, page 42.

Goldstein, Helen Fried Kirshblum, "Turkey: A haven for Jews in times of storm," *Women's League Outlook*, 63(3):17, Spring 1993.

Gross, Carol Cott, "Coffee and custom," *Inside*, 11(1):184, Spring 1990.

Hazard, Patrick D., "Focus: Infamous anniversary," *Jewish Exponent*, Dec. 30, 1994, page 3.

Hochberg, Ilene, "Fashion figures," *Inside*, 11(4):62, Winter 1990.

"In Brief: Indyk confirmed as an ambassador," *Jewish Exponent*, March 10, 1995, page 4.

Jackson, James O., "More than remembrance," *Time*, Feb. 6, 1995, pages 36–40.

Kaplan, Rachel, "French Jewry 50 years after the deportations," *Inside*, 16(2):40, Summer 1995.

Keating, Douglas J., "For Bikel, 27 years on 'Roof,'" *Philadelphia Inquirer*, Nov. 21, 1994, page D1.

Kent, Bill, "The krav maga kid," *Inside*, 12(1):52, Spring 1991.

"Kiryat Shmoneh symbolizes Israel's fighting spirit," *Palm Beach Jewish Journal Israeli Independence Day Supplement*, May 2–8, 1995, page 9.

Kranz, Hezki, "Coming of age," *JNF Illustrated*, Spring 1994, pages 27–28.

Landau, David, "In Casablanca, Jews in harmony with Muslims," *Jewish Exponent*, Dec. 2, 1994, page 9-X.

Laub, Karin, "Austrian decries Holocaust," *Philadelphia Inquirer*, Nov. 16, 1994, page A8.

Ledger, Martha, "Morocco bound," *Inside*, 15(4):65, Winter 1994.

Lehmann-Haupt, Christopher, "Books of the Times: Cutting a myth down to human size," *New York Times*, July 14, 1994, page C16.

Levenson, Gabriel, "Jewish sites of Boston," *Jewish Exponent*, July 21, 1995, page 6-X.

Longman, Jere, "Skater brings Israel to the Games," *New York Times*, Feb. 8, 1994, page B14.

"Loose talk," *Palm Beach Jewish Times*, Feb. 17, 1995, page 11.

Luxner, Larry, "Virgin Island synagogue," *Jewish Exponent*, Nov. 18, 1994, page 6-X.

"Masada inspires Israelis with ancient tale of heroism," *Palm Beach Jewish Journal Israeli Independence Day Supplement*, May 2–8, 1995, page 33.

Mayer, Paul Yogi, "The great deception: A personal recollection of Hitler's Olympic Games, 1936," *Jewish Quarterly*, 39(2):41–46, Summer 1992.

Mazel, Michelle, "Quality of environment: The greening of Israel," *Jerusalem Post Magazine*, June 17, 1994, page 20.

"Milestones: Stepping down," *Time*, Jan. 30, 1995, page 21.

Murphy, Richard. "Israeli rabbi recalls Buchenwald liberation," *Philadelphia Inquirer*, April 10, 1995, page A10.

Naftalin, Robin, "Two genealogical resources at the Keren Kayemeth," *Avotaynu*, 10(2):38, Summer 1994.

"News & information," *Sky Magazine*, 23(2):17, February 1994.

"Newsmakers," *Philadelphia Inquirer*, April 9, 1994, page D13.

"Newsmakers," *Philadelphia Inquirer*, Aug. 28, 1994, page A3.

"Obituaries: Shlomo Carlebach, rabbi, songwriter," *Jewish Exponent*, Oct. 28, 1994, page 73.

"Obituary: Shlomo Goren; rabbi was strong PLO critic," *Philadelphia Inquirer*, Oct. 30, 1994, page B6.

"Perspectives 1994," *Newsweek*, Dec. 26, 1994–Jan. 2, 1995, page 68.

Robinson, Abby, "Almost paradise," *Inside*, 14(1):42, Spring 1993.

Rottenberg, Dan, "The 'Jackie Robinson of Jewish academia,' " *Inside*, 16(1):64, Spring 1995.

Rubin, Jeff, "The lowdown on lulavs and etrogs," *Jewish Monthly*, 109(1):12, August–September 1994.

Sacharow, Fredda, "Memorial milestone," *Jewish Exponent*, Nov. 4, 1994, page 20.

Sacharow, Fredda, comp., "News Ex-Press: Shh! Don't spill the beans," *Jewish Exponent*, Sept. 15, 1995, page 9.

Sacharow, Fredda, comp., "News Ex-Press: Wet and wild: Israeli athletes dripping with pride," *Jewish Exponent*, Aug. 1, 1996, page 8.

"Safed was the 'miracle' of the 1948 war," *Palm Beach Jewish Journal Israeli Independence Day Supplement*, May 2–8, 1995, page 6.

"Shabbat policy to stay," *Jewish Exponent*, June 16, 1995, page 59.

Siegal, Marcia, "Recalling one man's role," *Jewish Exponent*, Oct. 7, 1994, page 22.

Silverstein, Marilyn, "Two centuries of change: Rodeph Shalom kicks off bicentennial year," *Jewish Exponent*, Oct. 7, 1994. page 4-X.

Simons, Marlise, "Chirac affirms France's guilt in fate of Jews," *New York Times*, July 17, 1995, page A1.

Smukler, Joseph, "20 years after Jackson-Vanik, senator is fondly remembered," *Jewish Exponent*, Jan. 20, 1995, page 5.

Staub, Molly Arost, "Jews of the Emerald Isle," *Jewish Exponent*, Jan. 6, 1995, page 1-X.

Stieglitz, Maria, "Beach, sun and surf, but no boardwalk," *Jewish Exponent*, March 31, 1995, page 6-X.

Strasser, Teresa, "For wounded gold medalist, kudos and a 'mi shebeirakh,' " *Jewish Exponent*, Aug. 1, 1996, page 25.

"Torch runner to link Israel and Philadelphia," *Jewish Exponent*, Dec. 2, 1994, page 12.

"Transition," *Newsweek*, Aug. 7, 1995, page 45.

Valdes, Lesley, "On music: String music of uncommon affirmation," *Philadelphia Inquirer*, May 2, 1995, page E1.

Wesolowski, Amy, ed., "Insiders," *Inside*, 15(4):12, Winter 1994.

Organizations

Source material was generously provided by the following organizations.

American Committee for the Weizmann Institute of Science

American Friends of the Hebrew University

American Jewish Historical Society

American Red Magen David for Israel

American Society for Technion

Beth Sholom Congregation, Elkins Park, Pa.

Congregation Shearith Israel, New York

El Al Israel Airlines Ltd.

Embassy of Israel

Hadassah

Hebrew Union College–Jewish Institute of Religion

The Jewish Museum, New York

Jewish National Fund

National Museum of American Jewish History, Philadelphia

Society of Friends of Touro Synagogue

United States Holocaust Memorial Museum

United Synagogue of Conservative Judaism

University of Judaism

Women's League for Conservative Judaism

Yeshiva University

YIVO Institute for Jewish Research

Other Sources

Burns, Ken. *Baseball,* PBS mini-series, episode #5, originally broadcast Sept. 22, 1994.

Groner, Judyth, and Madeline Wikler, *My Very Own Jewish Calendar,* 5754. Rockville, Md., Kar-Ben Copies, 1993.

"In the Beginning: American Judaica from the Collection of Dr. A.S.W. Rosenbach," Rosenbach Museum and Library, Philadelphia, January 1995.

"Masters of the 20th Century," Circle Gallery, San Francisco, July 1995.

"Mosaic: Jewish Life in Florida," National Museum of American Jewish History, Philadelphia, November 1994.

Program notes, *Joel Grey: Borscht Capades '94.* Royal Poinciana Playhouse, Palm Beach, Fla., February 1994.

Resource: A Directory of Jewish Life in Palm Beach County. Palm Beach Jewish Journal, 1994.